CHRISTIAN
BASICS

SAINT **SHENOUDA**PRESS

CHRISTIAN BASICS

- Fr Kyrillos Farag -

ST SHENOUDA'S PRESS
SYDNEY, AUSTRALIA
2021

Christian Basics
Fr Kyrillos Farag

COPYRIGHT © 2021
St Shenouda Press

All rights reserved. Except for brief quotations in critical publications or reviews, no part of this book may be reproduced in any manner without prior written permission from the publisher.

ST SHENOUDA PRESS
8419 Putty Rd,
Putty, NSW, 2330

www.stshenoudapress.com

ISBN 13: 978-0-6488658-8-9

All scripture quotations, unless otherwise indicated, are taken from the New King James Version®. Copyright © 1982 by Thomas Nelson, Inc. Used by permission. All rights reserved.

Edited by: Dr. Kirollos Nassief

Contents

Introduction	7
Fruits of the Life with God	15
The Beatitudes	85
The Orthodox Creed	107
Introduction to the Coptic Orthodox Church	117
The Holy Sacraments	121
How to Confess?	127
Saints and Martyrs Inspire the Faith Today	131
Raising Children to be Children of God	137
Monasticism	145

Introduction

Who is Jesus Christ?

The Orthodox Christian faith does not begin with proofs for the existence of God, but is rather founded upon God's revelation of Himself, most especially in the incarnation of Jesus Christ.

The incarnation of Jesus, the term used to describe when God became Man, occupies a central position in the teaching of the church. According to the Orthodox faith, Jesus is much more than a pious man or a profound teacher of morality. In Him, the divinity of God is perfectly united with humanity. That is, He is fully God and fully human, without a compromise of either entity.

Jesus' desire to reveal both who He is and our identity in Him permeates the Gospels, especially when He asks His disciples, "But who do you say that I am?"

(Matt 16:15). In response, Simon Peter, one of His disciples, answers saying, "You are the Christ, the Son of the living God." (Matt 16:16)

He in fact declared this about Himself through various words and signs. One example of this was when He said to the Jews, "Most assuredly, I say to you, before Abraham was, I AM" (John 8:58). One may wonder why the very next verse says, "Then they took up stones to throw at Him" (John 8:59). In order to further understand this, a glance at the Old Testament is required, where we find Moses the Prophet enquiring of God regarding His name, to which He responds, "'I AM WHO I AM.' And He said, "Thus you shall say to the children of Israel, 'I AM has sent me to you'" (Exodus 3:14). The Jews well-acquainted with Scripture and knowing that God refers to Himself as "I AM", accused Jesus of blasphemy saying He was "making Himself equal with God" (John 5:18). This also reveals that Jesus, as God, has no beginning and that it was He that was speaking with Abraham, Moses and the rest of the Prophets centuries before His incarnation. It is also He that is present in our lives today!

My Identity in Jesus

Jesus reveals the nature of God further by also completing His name from being, "I AM", to referring to Himself saying, "I AM the bread of life", "I AM the light of the world", "I AM the good shepherd" and "I AM the way, the truth, and the life". These are only a few of the references, wherein Jesus reveals that our whole identity and our entire being lie in Him.

The beauty lies in the fact that Jesus is more than just our God, but is also our Friend, Comforter and the One whom we love wholeheartedly due to the great love He first bestows upon each of us.

This can be extracted from both the personal experiences of those who accepted the invitation, "Taste and see that the Lord is good" (Psalm 34:8) as well as through His interactions with various individuals as recounted by the Gospels. Without exception, all individuals who met Jesus with an open heart had their lives transformed, from being characterised by insecurity to being filled with peace, from misery to joy, from unguided to purpose-driven, from loneliness to love and from death to life.

> *JESUS IS MORE **than just our God, but is also our Friend, Comforter and the One whom we love***

In the Gospel of John, Chapter 4, we read of Jesus' interaction with a woman from a city called Samaria who was despised by her community. She was a woman with a corrupt reputation of having married five different men, something that not even society would promote at that time. So much so, that she would travel at midday in the scorching heat of the sun to fill her waterpot, a time that no one else would, in order to avoid the judgement people would heap on her. Jesus, however, left all and travelled for hours on foot in the same heat to meet this one woman, not a multitude, but one individual who needed healing. Christ desired to communicate to her that her identity and self-worth are not dictated by what people think of her, nor by her occupation, nor by the mistakes she previously made – but by the fact that she is loved by Him as a loving Father and Friend regardless of her past. Her life was transformed from this interaction in which she observed the sweetness of Jesus, to the extent that she joyfully left her waterpot, went her way into the city, and said to the very people she was avoiding, *"Come, see a Man who told me all things that I ever did. Could this be the Christ?"* (John 4:29)

Chapter 3 of the Gospel of John then presents a character by the name of Nicodemus who, unlike the Samaritan woman, was not a social outcast but rather a prominent leader of the Jews, indicating that he was wealthy and educated. In modern times, he would have been equivalent to an Oxford scholar or a rich entrepreneur. In a world where it can be thought that successful and socially prominent people have no need for God, this notion is quickly challenged by Nicodemus' encounter with Jesus. He approached Jesus by night, for fear of ridicule by the Jews, and had a lengthy discussion with Him. He was attracted to Jesus, after realising that His temporary status and riches were not enough to satisfy him, nor were they sufficient to fill the void in his identity. He desired something more meaningful, needed something (or someone) more profound. The eyes of his heart became directed towards Jesus, whom he discovered provides real meaning and true purpose to his existence . We read later on in Chapter 19 that this same Nicodemus became a devoted follower of Jesus, to the point that he gave up his riches in service to Him after His death on the cross, in the form of costly ointments.

These experiences are countless and epitomised by the image of Jesus on the cross. His arms are stretched wide open, to warmly accept both the poor and the rich, the weak and the strong. He invites everyone to come to the knowledge of the truth and discover their true identity, which lies in Him.

The two encounters described earlier reveal that Jesus became all in all for both the Samaritan woman and Nicodemus. To every person, Jesus satisfies their own individual need. We read elsewhere that He is a Physician to those who are sick, even for those who were without hope such as the blind, crippled and leprous. Death itself was not an obstacle for Him, as seen in various instances including when He had compassion on the grieving family of a man named Lazarus and raised him from the dead. He is moreover a Teacher to the simple, who placed great emphasis on educating the multitudes concerning the meaning of authentic human life and the interpretation of the Scriptures. He is also a Friend, given that He frequently addressed His disciples as friends.

What makes all these attributes of Jesus more meaningful and personal is that ultimately He is indeed also God! Imagine that! God Himself, the Creator of the universe, calls YOU His friend and His son.

Of further significance is the fact that the name Jesus can be translated as 'Saviour'. His death on the cross was an act of redemption, an act of rescue, an act of reconciliation and an act of renewal for humanity. Through His death, He conquered the power of sin and death, and through His resurrection from the dead, He opened to us the door to eternal life. The extreme pain of the cross and the torture that preceded it was no match for His desire that we be rescued from death and corruption, and live eternally with Him in the Kingdom of Heaven.

Our identity therefore does not lie in people's opinions, social status or riches, which are all temporary, but in the love of Jesus which is unwavering and eternal.

Living Out a Relationship with Jesus

Given the sweetness of Jesus, His evident love for us and the reality of His presence today, the question then follows, how can we begin a relationship with Him? Just like the foundation for building a relationship with anyone else is to spend time with them, the same principal applies here. We are to spend time in His presence through prayer, reading His Word in the Bible and participating in the Sacraments of the church.

Through prayer, we speak to Him, offering Him words of praise and thanksgiving for His great love, telling Him about our sorrows and troubles, and receiving joy and answers to our requests. Through reading the Bible, we hear the voice of Jesus as He sends us personal messages and we gain a greater understanding of who He is and who we are in relation to Him. Through participating in the Sacraments and life of the church, we participate in the resurrection of Jesus through Baptism, become a new person through Repentance and Confession, and gain the gift of eternal life through Eucharist. Life with Jesus is thus one founded on love, where we love Him because He first loved us.

> *LIFE WITH JESUS is thus one founded on love, where we love Him because He first loved us.*

Fruits of the Life with God

A life with God brings forth many fruits, giving it meaning, purpose and beauty. Moreover, it brings forth virtues, summarised by St. Paul as he says,

> "But the fruit of the Spirit is love, joy, peace, longsuffering, kindness, goodness, faithfulness, gentleness, self-control." (Galatians 5:22-23)

The fruit of the Spirit mentioned here is the virtue that results from a synergy between our own spiritual struggle and the growth of grace from God. These fruits will be explored in more detail throughout this chapter, beginning with humility, which is the basis for all spiritual fruits.

Humility

It is difficult to talk about humility in the world we live in since people tend to think of another person's success as a threat to their own. People can fight and trick each other in order to maintain their positions and their status with no regard for the feelings of others.

Without humility, however, it is very difficult to see what is in our hearts and what it is God is trying to show us.

Humility is not something we are born with but rather comes from God and our choice to follow His commandants. Many of us strive to attain humility but fail continually for two reasons. Namely, we are pressing towards attaining this virtue whilst relying on our own efforts to do so, and moreover because the life we live is not compatible with what we are trying to achieve. We therefore end up failing.

So, what is humility? And how can we gain it?

St Paul writes concerning Christ,

> *"Let this mind be in you which was also in Christ Jesus, who, being in the form of God, did not consider it robbery to be equal with God, but made Himself of no reputation, taking the form of a bondservant, and coming in the likeness of men. And being found in*

appearance as a man, He humbled Himself and became obedient to the point of death, even the death of the cross" (Philippians 2:5-8)

It is pivotal to realise that the epitome of humility is what Christ did, who, being God, emptied Himself and came in the likeness of men. This is true humility. However, when we aim towards humility, we are rather realising our true selves, as mere humans.

God blesses the person who holds everything with an open hand, not allowing anything to impede their service to God and their obedience to His teachings. Such a person displays humility, as they deny themselves and realise that nothing in the world is as valuable as Christ Jesus.

Some characteristics of a humble person may include:

- ❖ Not doing things with the intention of receiving praise and glorification from others
- ❖ Utilising their talents for the glory of God
- ❖ Adopting the life of praise and thanksgiving
- ❖ Dedicating time and energy to assist others where needed

We read in 2 Chronicles 7:14,

"If My people who are called by My name will humble themselves, and pray and seek My face, and turn from their wicked ways, then

> *I will hear from heaven, and will forgive their sin and heal their land."*

This verse reveals to us the value of humility in God's eyes, for nothing is more repulsive than a proud and arrogant heart. God, however, does not strictly wait for us to do all the things mentioned in the verse above in order to bless us. He knows our heart and our intention before we even take one step towards humility and righteousness. As soon as He sees our desire to attain humility, He sends grace and divine support to help us reach it. For every step we take towards God, He takes 100 steps towards us.

There is a story of a King called Ahab which clearly shows us the mercy of God towards everyone, both the good and the evil. The story starts when King Ahab desired the land next door to his royal house in Northern Israel. He was willing to pay a sum of money to get hold of it but Naboth, the owner, refused to sell the land as it was the inheritance of his fathers. King Ahab was displeased by this and so his wife Jezebel decided to take matters into her own hands by plotting against Naboth. She wrote a letter to the elders arranging for false witnesses to accuse him of having blasphemed against God and the King. He was therefore stoned and killed, thereby allowing King Ahab to claim the land he desired.

God spoke to a prophet named Elijah stating that King Ahab would be punished for following Jezebel's advice and killing Naboth. When Elijah relayed the message and King Ahab heard those words, he quickly tore his clothes, covered himself in sackcloth, fasted and began to mourn his actions. Look then at God's response,

"And the word of the Lord came to Elijah the Tishbite, saying, 'See how Ahab has humbled himself before Me? Because he has humbled himself before Me, I will not bring the calamity in his days. In the days of his son I will bring the calamity on his house'" (1 Kings 21:28-29).

We can see how strongly humility moves the heart of God to compassion, as He says to Elijah, *"See how Ahab has humbled himself before Me?"* As a result of such humility, his punishment was withheld.

Truly, God's kindness is very great! He knew that King Ahab's heart was wicked, and yet He withheld judgement as soon as He witnessed his humility. Despite the trigger for King Ahab's humility being a fear of judgement, and having no real regard for God's commandments, God's

> *Despite our wickedness, God's grace and mercy is abundant and He readily forgives us when we offer a humble repentance.*

heart is still quickly moved to compassion at the sight of his mourning and humility.

What is even more interesting is that it is plausible to suggest that Ahab's repentance was temporary and not heartfelt. I say this since we read that he kept the land of Naboth, he did not rebuke his wife Jezebel, and he actually turned back to his old self in the following chapter.

What does this tell us? Despite our wickedness, God's grace and mercy is abundant and He readily forgives us when we offer a humble repentance. Nobody is exempt from God's mercy, regardless of how evil or sinful they are!

Keep the following words in your mind, *"God resists the proud, But gives grace to the humble"* (James 4:6). Therefore, humble yourself before the Lord that you may become pleasant to Him and attract His mercy and compassion.

Gentleness

Gentleness is a fruit of the Spirit in which one becomes characterised by meekness of personality and sensitivity to the needs of others. A Christian's gentle approach consistently puts them and those around them at peace.

St. Paul advised the early Christians,

> *"Therefore as the elect of God, holy and beloved, put on tender mercies, kindness, humbleness of mind, meekness, longsuffering; bearing with one another and forgiving one another, if anyone has a complaint against another, even as Christ forgave you, so you also must do"* (Colossians 3:12-13)

Moreover, Jesus says, *"learn from Me, for I am gentle and lowly in heart"* (Matthew 11:29). When Christ decided to describe Himself, He chose to highlight the importance of gentleness.

The early church fathers frequently associated the Holy Spirit with the virtue of gentleness. The Holy Spirit is of a sensitive essence, and greatly favours a gentle dwelling place that is free of turmoil. Hermas, a church elder from the 2nd century (c. 150 AD) once wrote,

"If any outburst of anger takes place in you, immediately the flame of the Holy Spirit, who is of a gentle nature begins to be quenched. For when He does not have a pure and calm place to dwell in, He seeks to depart."

St. Clement of Alexandria (c. 195 AD) also addressed the gentle nature of the Holy Spirit's descent during Christ's baptism as he wrote,

> *"When the Lord Jesus Christ was baptised, the Holy Spirit assumed the likeness of a dove, for He wished to declare His simplicity and majesty."*

The dove symbolises many virtues. It is white, denoting purity, and is also an elegant quiet bird, symbolising majesty. The dove's break into flight is soft with hardly a sound, symbolising the Spirit's gentle presence. It is a soft-spoken bird and does not attack other birds nor scavenge, highlighting the Spirit's tender approach in dealing with us.

The virtue of gentleness when abiding in a pure person or one that desires to be pure encourages slowness to wrath, which is itself a virtue. Anger derives from retaliation and spitefulness and is often swift and deliberate. The virtue of gentleness, however, helps develop the personality to be slow to anger and strengthens the capability of calming oneself and of thinking through situations where anger has erupted. In gentleness, one is taught to control their nerves and their tongue, and to use wisdom in responding to provocative people and situations.

The Old Testament Book of Proverbs warns, "An angry man stirs up strife, and a furious man abounds in transgression" (Proverbs 29:22).

St James, the first bishop of Jerusalem, instructed the Christians abroad, "So then, my beloved brethren, let every man be swift to hear, slow to speak, slow to wrath" (James 1:19).

He furthers this point by explaining that gentleness is the mark of true wisdom as he writes,

"For where envy and self-seeking exist, confusion and every evil thing are there. But the wisdom that is from above is first pure, then peaceable, gentle, willing to yield, full of mercy, and good fruits, without partiality and without hypocrisy" (James 3:13-17)

Even when admonishing someone for their wrong doings, even this should be done with gentleness as St Paul says, "Brethren, if a man is overtaken in any trespass, you who are spiritual restore such a one in a spirit of gentleness, considering yourself lest you also be tempted" (Galatians 6:1).

In the Holy Bible, gentleness is also a sign of inner beauty as it says,

"Do not let your adornment be merely outward—arranging the hair, wearing gold, or putting on fine apparel—rather let it be

> *the hidden person of the heart, with the incorruptible beauty of a gentle and quiet spirit, which is very precious in the sight of God"* (I Peter 3:3)

Gentleness is indeed a fruit of the Spirit which itself allows the Holy Spirit to dwell within us. It is the trait of those living in Heaven and is capable of saving us from the sin of anger.

Faith

Faith is more than just the five-letter word that spells it. There are two aspects to it. There is the willingness to believe and trust that God cares about each of us and is with us each day, and then there is the strong conviction in the person of Christ and His teachings. Faith does not have a simple definition, though, but is rather an on-going process of constant learning, growing, failure, restoration, and empowerment. It takes effort and stamina to build faith. It takes courage to fail and rise up, persistence to attack negative thoughts and defend true precepts. It is a commitment to live out what we believe, a call to represent our belief, to live wisely, and above all to remain true to the Lord Jesus Christ.

Building a strong and mature faith requires us to start at the bottom and work our way up. In today's world, society encourages us to start a job as fast as possible and leave the preparation to be done simultaneously along the way, if it is done at all. We are indoctrinated to start as close to the top of the ladder as possible and that it is okay to miss a few steps. This, however, does not work in the case of building a strong faith and commitment to the Lord Jesus Christ.

Firstly, we must learn to trust in God. The Lord Jesus Christ often rebuked His disciples for their lack of faith. He wanted them to completely trust Him in the simpler and less significant issues of life, so that they could fathom the glorious Resurrection which would come later on.

They were individually called to follow Christ, travelled with Him and were privileged to hear His teachings firsthand. They also had multiple personal experiences where He provided in time of need, as in the miracle of the 5 loaves and 2 fish which fed 5000 men and their families. If we read the gospel account of this miracle carefully, we realise that it says there were 12 baskets filled with the leftover fragments. Was this a coincidence, given there were also 12 disciples? Surely not! The Lord wanted them to walk home with a reminder of what they witnessed, as a source of strengthening of their faith.

There was once a man who brought his ill son to Christ for healing. During which the following interaction takes place,

> *"Jesus said to him, 'If you can believe, all things are possible to him who believes.' Immediately the father of the child cried out and said with tears, 'Lord, I believe; help my unbelief!'"* (Mark 9:19-24)

The conversation gives us a beautiful prayer which we can say ourselves at times of doubt, *"Lord, I believe; help my unbelief!"*

The second step in the ladder of faith, is the formation of a strong belief in the Lord Jesus Christ and His teachings. Humility, which we discussed earlier, plays an integral role here in the development of such faith as we need to put our ego aside and accept what He says. When we also believe the goodness of Christ, and His sweet intention toward us, we can more easily accept His teachings, knowing that it is in our best interest.

There is another incident in which a centurion believes wholeheartedly that Christ has the power to heal his servant by uttering just one word, without even entering his house or touching the man.

> *"The centurion answered and said, 'Lord, I am not worthy that You should come under my roof. But only speak a word, and my servant*

will be healed. For I also am a man under authority, having soldiers under me. And I say to this one, 'Go,' and he goes; and to another, 'Come,' and he comes; and to my servant, 'Do this,' and he does it.' When Jesus heard it, He marveled, and said to those who followed, 'Assuredly, I say to you, I have not found such great faith, not even in Israel!'" (Matthew 8:8-10)

This faith definitely stemmed from the Lord's teachings that He is *"the way, the truth and the life"* (John 14:6), and again when He says, *"Come to Me, all you who labor and are heavy laden, and I will give you rest"* (Matthew 11:28). The man must have believed these words and so ran to Christ without hesitation.

The step following that is, once a strong belief in the Lord Jesus Christ develops within us, we must be Biblically literate to reinforce our beliefs both personally and for others we will encounter. One cannot play a sport if they do not understand the rules or cannot refer back to them when they are challenged. Similarly, we cannot defend our faith if we do not understand it, and thus we must spend quality time reading the Bible.

> *WE CANNOT DEFEND our faith if we do not understand it, and thus we must spend quality time reading the Bible.*

The Lord Christ admonished one of His disciples, Simon Peter, who would later on deny Him the morning of His crucifixion,

"And the Lord said, 'Simon, Simon! Indeed, Satan has asked for you, that he may sift you as wheat. But I have prayed for you, that your faith should not fail; and when you have returned to Me, strengthen your brethren" (Luke 22:31-32).

He then instructs him to strengthen the brethren once he has returned to Him. What does this mean? Simply, there will be times in which our faith will weaken, but it is at this stage in which we need to run to Him for support. We will then arise with a renewed faith capable of refreshing and strengthening those around us also.

The next point of ascension on the ladder of faith is a call to action and commitment to the Lord Jesus Christ in our daily lives, since faith without execution becomes futile. This does not mean that we will never sin or fall short again. No, on the contrary, there will be failures, but our commitment to Christ means that we learn from them, pick ourselves up, and become stronger. For example, if we are

> *There will be failures, but our commitment to Christ means that we learn from them, pick ourselves up, and become stronger*

trying to overcome a particular bad habit for the sake of Christ, or acquire a particular virtue such as gentleness, we ought not to be disheartened if we find ourselves trying and yet failing.

St. Peter is a good example for us of someone who made mistakes but eventually matured in faith as he learned from them. On one end of his life we see him denying Christ before His crucifixion, and then on the other end we see him being imprisoned and martyred for his faith in Christ.

Again using St. Peter as an example, there was a time in which he walked on water for a distance after Christ called him towards Him outside the boat, Himself standing on water. However, when he began to doubt, he began to drown instead. He started strong but his faith faltered and so it was not mature enough yet for the deed. Many remember his 'drowning faith' rather than realising that he is most probably the only man, other than Jesus, to have ever walked upon water. Although his faith was not perfect, and he doubted and began to drown, look at how strong the faith he started off with was and how much stronger it would become as the days and years went by.

St. Peter was thus, like us, a long-term work in progress. He was often humiliated by his lack of faith, often hesitant to challenge his faith for fear of failure, but when he did fail and recover from it, he was more effective than ever in the service of the Lord Jesus Christ.

Failures of faith should thus be viewed as challenges because the fact of the matter is that we are all going to fail, as it is part of our human nature. We all fall short of the glory of God. No matter how gifted one may be, no matter how committed they are, no matter how many friends they have, they are still prone to failure. Failure does not elude anyone, particularly when it comes to faith. Failure is certainly humbling but should never be seen as finality.

The next step is the calling to be prepared at all times and in all places to face Christ in His second coming. There are two parables which Christ taught concerning this,

"But know this, that if the master of the house had known what hour the thief would come, he would have watched and not allowed his house to be broken into. Therefore you also be ready, for the Son of Man is coming at an hour you do not expect" (Matthew 24:43-44).

"Then the kingdom of heaven shall be likened to ten virgins who took their lamps and went out to meet the bridegroom. Now five of them were wise, and five were foolish. Those who were foolish took their lamps and took no oil with them, but the wise

Fruits of the Life with God

took oil in their vessels with their lamps. But while the bridegroom was delayed, they all slumbered and slept" (Matthew 25:1-5).

Both of these parables point to the same message, whether it is to "watch" in the first passage or to "collect oil" in the second one, we are called to be ready! Christ's second coming, that is, the end of life on Earth and the beginning of the one in Heaven may occur at any time, and so our faith should be geared towards this mindset.

As we progress up the ladder, there comes the need to pray for stronger faith.

"So Jesus said to them, 'Because of your unbelief; for assuredly, I say to you, if you have faith as a mustard seed, you will say to this mountain, 'Move from here to there,' and it will move; and nothing will be impossible for you.'" (Matthew 17:20).

This actually took place historically through the faith of a simple man called St. Simon the Tanner in the 6th century, in which the El-Mouttem Mountain physically moved after 3 days of prayer and fasting by the entire church (in response to threats of persecution by Islamic leaders after attacking the legitimacy of the above verse).

Do we have this kind of faith? If not, then we must pray for it!

In the story of David and Goliath, David had faith that the Lord was on his side and that he could thus defeat Goliath despite the vast difference in size and physical might. At the time when a paralysed man was brought to the Lord Jesus Christ by his four friends, their faith was not weakened by the opposition from the huge crowds surrounding them, rather they maintained their strong faith and the man was healed by Him. The woman who reached out to touch the hem of the Lord Jesus Christ's cloak after having a flow of blood for 12 years knew that she would be ridiculed for doing so, but her faith was unshaken and so she was healed. All these accounts in addition to so many more have one common theme: they are examples of people who had a deep trust that all things are possible with the Lord. This is the kind of faith we need, that we must pray for!

The fact that Christ says if you have faith as small as a mustard seed you can move mountains, as quoted above, means that the most difficult of missions can be carried out with the smallest of faith. What seems as overwhelming and insurmountable as a mountain top can be overcome by a little faith.

Origen (245 AD), a 3rd century church elder, says referring to the same verse above,

> *"The mountains here spoken of are, in my opinion, the hostile powers that have their being in a flood of great wickedness ...*

Whenever, then, anyone has all faith so that he no longer disbelieves in any things that are contained in the Holy Scripture ... he has all faith as a grain of mustard seed."

Thus, he relates such powerful faith to believing all that the Scripture (ie. the Bible) says.

In summary, one faithful servant of God can make a difference to the start of a person on their journey of faith. One spiritual convention of faithful attendees can make a difference in the life of a weaker person. One whose faith needed strengthening that was encouraged to attend the praises at church may end up praising God throughout the remainder of their life. Even one candle lit in a church liturgy could brighten the path of a sinner.

> ONE CANDLE LIT *in a church liturgy could brighten the path of a sinner*

Faith is in fact the essence of our life, as St. Paul writes, *"For in it the righteousness of God is revealed from faith to faith; as it is written, 'The just shall live by faith'"* (Romans 1:17). The importance of faith in the spiritual life is further underscored by St. Clement of Alexandria who once said, *"We have discovered faith to be the first movement towards salvation."*

It is my prayer that through perseverance, persistence, vigilance and the grace of God we grow and mature in faith, and therefore enjoy a beautiful relationship with the Lord Jesus Christ.

Goodness

It is important as we continue to address the fruits of the Holy Spirit, to remember what it is that is implied by the word 'fruit'. It is first given to us in its original form as a seed and then left up to us to plant and nurture and allow to grow.

This is different from a God given gift in which lies a talent or particularly desirable human trait that we can readily use.

Regarding the fruit of 'goodness', it is one with many far reaching sprouts.

St Paul writes, *"As we have therefore the opportunity, let us do good unto all men"* (Galatians 6:10).

We are instructed to do good to all people. This does not mean to repay someone who wronged us with another wrong. If someone decides they are not going to speak to us, should we not speak to them either? If someone steals our money, would we steal it back? If someone tells a lie against us, would we fabricate a lie about them also? Did this manner of behaviour ever instil goodness in a person?

Fruits of the Life with God

What makes a person good though? What helps a person remain steadfast in goodness?

The answer lies in Psalm 1:3, in which we are told that the person filled with goodness is, *"like a tree planted by the rivers of water."* That is, just like a tree is nourished by the water of the riverbank, we likewise are nourished with goodness from the source of goodness Himself, God!

The Holy Bible uses many illustrations as such to teach us that the good in a person must come from God, be allowed to grow, and be protected from evil influences. Christ teaches us to *"Bless those who curse you, do good to those who hate you, and pray for those who spitefully use you and persecute you"* (Matthew 5:44). We thus see here that Christ's standard of goodness is different to that of the world. We are called to something higher, a goodness that is unconditional and shown even to our enemies.

Goodness always trumps evil. It is a God-like trait and so we can be confident of its fortitude in our lives. Can you ever remember a time in your life when goodness did not ultimately win? Rest assured that if you are shunned or mistreated for your goodness, that you will eventually win those people over. If you hold steadfast to your beliefs and remain faithful in prioritising God in your life, you will ultimately be held in high regard for that.

Even if you are going through a tough time, you will still triumph if you take on the fruit of goodness. A crown of glory will follow the struggle and initial bitterness you are facing.

We read in the book of Romans,

> *"Do not be overcome by evil, but overcome evil with good"* (Romans 12:21)

St Paul here confirms the power of goodness, instructing us to maintain it even in the face of evil. We should not be occupied, however, with labelling others evil or good. Our focus should rather be on desiring to reflect God's goodness and being a light to the world such that all may see the *"good works and glorify [our] Father in Heaven"* (Matthew 5:16).

It is my prayer that as St. Paul taught, that we all strive to live a fruitful life of goodness and that we do "not grow weary while doing good" and that *"as we have opportunity, let us do good to all"* (Galatians 6:9-10).

Kindness

In the gospels we read of a parable of a vineyard and the stewards working therein. Our Lord Jesus Christ describes Himself as the Vine and us as the branches. Trees, green pastures and vineyards are often used in the Holy Bible to symbolically represent life and growth. Thus Christ uses the example of the vine to help us realise that the fruits of the Spirit we have

Fruits of the Life with God

been discussing stem from the life that the Vine, Christ Himself, provides to the branches. This section now deals with the fruit of kindness.

Kindness is an offshoot of the branch bearing the fruit of love. Kindness starts first and foremost in the heart and is translated in thoughts, words and actions. The book of Proverbs describes a kind tongue saying, *"The tongue of the righteous is choice silver; the heart of the wicked is worth little"* (Proverbs 10:20). We also read, *"The lips of the righteous know what is acceptable, but the mouth of the wicked what is perverse"* (Proverbs 10:32). So, what is the opposite of kindness?

The opposite of kindness is hatred. The expression "I hate you" is unfortunately frequently and liberally used. Those who say "I hate you" to their parents or siblings are developing a deep-seated problem in their personality. It is both wrong and unhealthy. Hating one another is not alluded to anywhere in the Holy Bible as being acceptable or beneficial in any way. It is doubtless that hating one another is wrong. The only proper hatred that the Holy Bible recommends and teaches is the hatred of sin.

Therefore, pronouncing hatred onto parents, siblings or anyone is committing a very sinful act because it is pronouncing hatred on people as opposed to pronouncing it on their wrong acts. Choosing kindness as a response for a hurtful act outlasts hatred by far.

The Lord hated sin but not sinners. Kindness defuses hate and affects people's sinful nature. It serves as the most appropriate thing to demonstrate in any given situation and is proven both psychologically and physically to be the healthiest thing to do.

Research shows an association between hatred and bitterness and many physical complaints in the long run including headaches, heart disease, and somatic pain. In addition, hatred increases our internal stress level, which overtime has the cumulative effect of leading to premature aging. Thus, the consequences of hatred are many. Instead, our Lord teaches us that prayer is the most effective act of kindness towards our opponents, as He says,

> *"Love your enemies, bless those who curse you, do good to those who hate you, and pray for those who spitefully use you and persecute you"* (Matthew 5:44)

The Lord Jesus Christ whilst on Earth was the epitome of kindness, through which He was capable of making the common person feel special, the unbeliever believe, and the unrighteous desire righteousness. The Lord Jesus Christ showed much kindness to others, did many good things to the unfortunate and cared for the poor and those suffering. Through His enduring loving kindness He neither boasted of His self-worth, nor ridiculed the weak, or belittled the simple minded. Through His great kindness, not only

Fruits of the Life with God

did He relieve those who were burdened and heavy-laden with their challenging circumstances but also restored them and fortified them. We must therefore reflect the image of God who is all "merciful and gracious" (Exodus 34:6).

Christ's kindness must have overflowed and poured forth from Him as the sun radiates from heaven. His love and sweetness were renowned as His reputation preceded Him wherever He journeyed. The Lord Jesus Christ Himself said, *"I am the good shepherd; and I know My sheep, and am known by My own"* (John 10:14).

Thus, He knows our needs as His sheep, and through His kindness and favour, lavishly fulfils them. He is indeed good to us.

There are many symbolic inferences in the Holy Bible referring to the Lord Jesus Christ's kindness. For example, David the Psalmist wrote, *"Your rod and Your staff, they comfort me"* (Psalm 23:4).

> HE KNOWS OUR *needs as His sheep, and through His kindness and favour, lavishly fulfils them.*

A rod and a staff to the flock were a sign of the shepherd's care, guidance, and protection. Used correctly, they could be lifesaving instruments to all the sheep. The flock possibly comprised of different breeds, with some that were sickly and others that were disobedient; yet the rod and staff symbolised kindness, care and comfort to all of them.

The Lord Christ exhibited His loving kindness in every situation, as He encountered all despair and discouragement from people with His holy glance of compassion. He did just that for the woman with the flow of blood who by Jewish law was condemned as unclean and thus for twelve years labelled as an outcast, because of an illness incurred through most probably no fault of her own. She witnessed the Lord's kindness with others and so decided to overcome all obstacles and reach out to touch the hem of His cloak, with the faith she would be healed by Him. The Lord's kindness towards her was so great that He allowed Himself to be touched by her although she was viewed by everyone else as a curse. She was thus not only made well physically but also earned a strong faith that enabled her to become spiritually up lifted. The Lord had turned an outcast into a woman of great faith. The despicable woman with a bleeding disorder, an outcast of her own culture, would be a chosen example of the Lord's kind heart which would live on in history even after her departure.

Another example is the story of the blind man. He could not see the commotion nor the cause of the excitement around him before he was told Jesus was passing by. But could the blind man discern the voice

Fruits of the Life with God

of the Lord when he actually did pass by? Was it really the man's cry, *"Jesus ... have mercy on me"*, that caused Christ to stop walking and have him brought to Him? The man's voice would have been indiscernible amongst the large crowd! Moreover, how did the Lord happen to stop at just the right moment in His lengthy and unceasing travels to be able to meet the blind man? There is only one possible explanation, and that being the Lord's kindness. It was the kindness that could be detected in His voice that allowed the blind man to recognise when He passed by and it was the Lord's foreknowledge and decision to heal the man that allowed Him to find him.

"So Jesus stood still and commanded him to be brought to Him. And when he had come near, He asked him, saying, 'What do you want Me to do for you?' He said, 'Lord, that I may receive my sight.' Then Jesus said to him, 'Receive your sight; your faith has made you well.' And immediately he received his sight, and followed Him, glorifying God. And all the people, when they saw it, gave praise to God" (Luke 18:40-43).

We see here that the Lord directly and purposefully asked the blind man about his request to which the blind man responded with a direct answer; he wanted back his physical sight.

The Lord's kindness, by giving sight to the blind man, naturally obliged him to then follow Him faithfully. His kindness had made a willing and heartfelt follower out of a blind man.

Other acts of kindness from Christ included preventing the stoning of a woman, addressing and honouring a tax collector who was hated by all as well as numerous other accounts in the gospels. In the latter, the sinful tax collector, whose name was Zacchaeus, was so overwhelmed by Christ's compassion that he decided to give half his goods to the poor, restoring fourfold to those he had taken from dishonestly.

It can be thus concluded that kindness, as was the case with Christ, can be heard in one's voice as well as seen on one's countenance. It is an old proverb that some people, however, are unable to see this kindness because of egotism, materialism, prejudice, greed, fear, love of power or revenge, and sometimes because of self-hate. As we saw above, the voice of kindness can induce someone to contemplate on the errors in their life and seek to correct them.

On another occasion, the Lord instructed Simon Peter to do works of kindness,

"So when they had eaten breakfast, Jesus said to Simon Peter, 'Simon, son of Jonah, do you love Me more than these?' He said to Him, 'Yes, Lord; You know that I love You.' He said to him, 'Feed My lambs'" (John 21:15).

Feeding His lambs would entail feeding the hungry, ministering to the sick and handicapped, visiting the neglected, caring for the homeless, loving the despised and spreading the Lord's love to all those who are willing to listen. All these things are considered acts of kindness. St. Peter entered into this experience of spreading Christ's love and kindness to others. He certainly did not expect himself to be preaching to non-believers later in his life, but courageously did so with a zeal for extending the Lord's loving kindness to all those who were in need.

Kindness affects people in different ways but it always touches their hearts. Let us pray to the Lord to grant us kind hearts that feel for people with love and not hatred. It must be noted that any act of mercy we perform is considered by the Lord as an act of kindness, even if this may be simply teaching or redirecting someone. It can change the lives of others and we should and can serve as the branch to produce the fruits of kindness in the lives of others today.

Patience

Everyone would like to add the virtue of patience to their personal attributes. Patience not only adds to our degree of spiritual fruitfulness but helps us to accomplish the most difficult of tasks with the least amount of effort. If we desire our lives to be fruitful and to have our hearts be conducive to hearing and obeying God's Word, this often happens with a patient ear. If we are complacent about hearing and obeying the Word of God, attaining fruits of the Spirit will be a constant problem in our lives. As the Scripture says,

> *"But he who received seed on the good ground is he who hears the word and understands it, who indeed bears fruit and produces: some a hundredfold, some sixty, some thirty"* (Matthew 13:23)

The seed in this parable represents the word of God, and so if a person keeps the word and obeys it with patience, it will spring forth into fruit.

Without such fruit, you will not achieve a fulfilling life but be in constant search of one instead. Many look toward support groups, self-help books, media outreach programs, and attachments to others for achieving a worldly optimal life style; often overlooking the spiritual seeds of God's Word and the application of Biblical truths to their lives. The fact of the matter is that support groups are transient parts of a mobile society, self-help advice changes almost daily, and attachment to others can sometimes be a source of frustration. God is the only stable source of security, ever present and unchanging, encouraging us to bear fruits which will ultimately enrich our life.

Fruits of the Life with God

Take caution when those around you tend to be impatient, have an on-going spirit of discontentment, a complaint of every sort, a negative attitude, and a detailed list of everything wrong happening in their life that they regularly converse about. Avoid these sorts of groups, meetings, and friends because it will encourage you to self-indulge in the negative behaviour as well. In an age of 'support systems' one must put God first in their time of need and as their ultimate source of support.

When things in life become difficult and hard to comprehend, we tend to desire a packaged solution that is readily available and mass produced. When things remain difficult and beyond our understanding for longer than we believe necessary, we tend to want to do something, anything, to take care of the problem. We may even wonder why God does not intervene and do something to rid us of our problem.

Patience is one of life's most desirable and sought-after fruits of the Holy Spirit. We often ask God for more patience in dealing with our problems. Sometimes in our pursuit of patience we think God may be testing us and this could absolutely be true. Testing a person is actually conducting an assessment to see the need for improvement in them. Don't we all need improvement in our earthly lives? On the other hand, the reverse may be true and we often find ourselves testing God, such as asking ourselves,

"Is He really there? Does He really care about me? Is He concerned about my life?"

God needs no testing. God is perfect; He is the measure of perfection against that which perfection is based upon. Therefore, God needs no improvement. So logically it does not make sense to even desire to test God by questioning His actions in our lives. Jesus said, "It is written again, 'You shall not tempt the LORD your God.'" (Matthew 4:7). We must believe that He knows what is best for each of us and therefore learn the usefulness of the fruit of patience.

When we think about what is upsetting our life circumstances with no apparent solution in sight, think about things in perspective. For example, why did the woman healed in Luke 13:11-12, have to suffer eighteen years with a spirit that had crippled her before she was healed by the Lord Jesus Christ? We read,

> *"And behold, there was a woman who had a spirit of infirmity eighteen years, and was bent over and could in no way raise her self up. But when Jesus saw her, He called her to Him and said to her, 'Woman, you are loosened from your infirmity'"* (Luke 13:11-12).

With increasing patience, a person learns to think in a positive manner rather than a confused or angry manner. Impatience generally does not lead to a solution, but simply causes a person to lose his inner peace. The person who has patience and thinks positively about what happens to him will think calmly and make his situation pass peacefully. The woman with the spirit for eighteen years glorified God when she was healed.

On the other hand, the person who cannot think positively but chooses to dwell on the negative aspects of things loses his patience, his thoughts become agitated and anxiety will cause his mind to be flooded with thoughts. The anxiety will increasingly build within the person and soon an outburst will occur. Not only outbursts of frustration emerge, but an anxious disposition develops that can be exhausting, spiritually troubling, and instils fear.

Nervous exhaustion can lead one to intolerance, preoccupation with their troubles in life and increased anxiety levels. Again, with the fruit of patience an endurance in all things and a release from stresses encompassing our daily lives is learned. Have you ever heard an eight-year-old say, "Boy am I stressed out"?

How can a child of eight years be stressed out? Perhaps he heard one of his parents saying this when they were younger. Being stressed out is a rather sad characteristic to imitate at such a young age. Rather they should have heard their parents say "faith and patient endurance can find a way"!

With patient endurance, four people brought a paralysed man to the Lord Jesus Christ to be healed.

> *"Then they came to Him, bringing a paralytic who was carried by four men. And when they could not come near Him because of the crowd, they uncovered the roof where He was. So when they had broken through, they let down the bed on which the paralytic was lying. When Jesus saw their faith, He said to the paralytic, 'Son, your sins are forgiven you.'"* (Mark 2:3-5).

The man had to be carried. The crowd to see the Lord Jesus had become so large it was overflowing out of the building. Most would have given up and said, "I can't." Patiently and calmly the four firmly believed the Lord Jesus Christ could heal their friend and they continued to think in an optimistic manner. Thinking positively, they went up the outdoor staircase and opened a hole in the roof. Through the hole they lowered their paralysed friend directly into the presence of the Lord.

The point is that when the four men encountered a great obstacle, which threatened the paralysed man's only chance of being healed, they did not see it as an insurmountable challenge but rather explored other entrances into the building. The over-crowded building and multitudes of on-lookers were not seen as a dead-end street but rather as the invitation to find another way to reach their destination.

Patience adheres to the "one step at a time" method. Take a step, then another step. With each step, have faith. "Moving mountains" is often a Biblical phrase that encourages people that with the smallest of faith they could move mountains. Patient enduring faith to overcome the insurmountable mountain or the hardest tasks in life can be accomplished with a desire to grow in faith, patience, and the trust that something positive can happen. Remember that all things are possible with God.

> *T<small>AKE A STEP</small>, **then another step**. With each step, have faith*

The Israelites did not have patience when leaving Egypt and following Moses into the desert. They were finally saved after their four-hundred-year bondage of servitude and yet still had the audacity to complain about lack of water and their desire to eat meat. So God provided them with water, with manna from Heaven (a special bread that was like white coriander seed and that tasted like wafers made with honey, as mentioned in Exodus 16:31) and with quail. They did not starve, nor succumb to thirst, and the Holy Bible even tells us that after fourty years of wandering in the desert that the very shoes on their feet did not wear out. Yet with all these provisions they continued to lack patience, still complained and were never content.

Perhaps we can all learn from the Israelites a valuable lesson in that patience is to, "in whatever state ... to be content. [To] know how to be abased and [to] know how to abound. Everywhere and in all things [to] have learned both to be full and to be hungry, both to abound and to suffer need" and to believe that "I can do all things through Christ who strengthens me" (Philippians 4:11-13).

This verse written by St. Paul gives us the key to possessing patience. We must believe in the authority of God and that through His strength we can overcome whatever life may bring.

May we all strive to be increasingly content in all things and anxious for nothing in handling the daily pressures of life; thereby bringing forth the perfect fruit of patience.

Peace

Peace has a special Biblical connotation. It is often called the son of faith. *"Therefore, having been justified by faith, we have peace with God through our Lord Jesus Christ"* (Romans 5:1).

Fruits of the Life with God

The Lord Jesus Christ is considered the 'King of Peace'. Being the truest source of peace known to man today, Christ, found no price great enough for peace and shed His own blood for its sake, *"Having made peace through the blood of His cross"* (Colossians 1:20).

Peace is considered one of the greatest gifts given to us in the Person of the Lord Jesus. To keep Him ever present in thought, the word peace was to become the Jewish word of custom to address both a greeting and a good-bye. Hence the importance of the word, 'salam', which means 'peace', since it reminded them of God's presence in everyday life. Today we continue to recite the words, *"Peace be with all"*, throughout the Divine Liturgy. They are said before the Prayer of Reconciliation, following the Creed and in many other parts of the liturgy. They are even the words the priest uses to dismiss the congregation at the conclusion by saying *"go in peace and may the peace of the Lord be with you all"*, after which the people leave in peace.

The Lord Jesus often spoke of the perfect peace reconciling humanity with God and that we are not to be afraid as a result. He said,

> *"Peace I leave with you, My peace I give to you; not as the world gives do I give to you. Let not your heart be troubled, neither let it be afraid"* (John 14:27)

This the Lord Jesus Christ spoke to His disciples concerning His eventual sequence of death including His Resurrection, Ascension into Heaven and Pentecost (the sending of the Holy Spirit). It further implies that peace is more than an earthly gift left behind, but a spiritual gift and an inheritance to the faithful.

This "peace be with you" message was to fill the disciples' hearts with such great peace, joy and comfort that they could not help but go out and spread such great news. As a result, lives would continue to be impacted some two thousand years later.

Peace was not only the message at the end of Christ's earthly life but it was the message present from the moment of His conception in the womb of the Virgin Mary at the beginning of His earthly life. The Archangel Gabriel said to St. Mary regarding the news that she would be the mother of the Lord Jesus Christ, "Do not be afraid, Mary, for you have found favour with God" (Luke 1:30). To further ensure peace, an Angel of the Lord said unto St. Joseph the Carpenter, "Joseph, son of David, do not be afraid to take to you Mary your wife, for that which is conceived in her is of the Holy Spirit" (Matthew 1:20). Both St. Mary and St. Joseph (through his wilful faith-inspired adoption) were to receive the ultimate Gift of Peace, Jesus Christ.

Fruits of the Life with God

The angels also announced to the lowly shepherds, "Do not be afraid, for behold, I bring you good tidings of great joy which will be to all people" (Luke 2:10). This was indeed THE night of peace, the birth of our Lord Jesus Christ. This verse is followed with, *"Glory to God in the Highest, and on earth, peace"* (Luke 2:14). When did peace come to earth except when the Lord Jesus Christ, the Son of God, was born? He came and brought His goodness and goodwill to all men.

The Lord Jesus Christ spoke these words to the disciples following His glorious resurrection, *"Why are you troubled? And why do doubts arise in your hearts?"* (Luke 24:38) This again reinforces that with peace there is no room for being afraid, no room for doubting and certainly no room for troubled hearts. Peace sparks joy and happiness in a person. There is no abounding negativity with peace. Only peacefulness brings us nearer to the Lord our God.

What is this peace of God and why is it connected most often to obliterating fear? Fear is present in most facets of life. We see homes with electronic alarm systems, learn of people owning guns in their homes and hear constant talk of war, bombings, and disruption of life in many parts of the world. People might ask, with such danger looming around us, is it not reasonable to be cautious and watchful? This is certainly needed, but alarm systems and guns do not deter fear. These are all desperate attempts at gaining peace but in fact are only superficial methods and not the real solution. True peace comes from the King of Peace, Jesus.

Many Biblical scholars today believe that the verse, *"I tell you not to resist an evil person. But whoever slaps you on your right cheek, turn the other to him also,"* (Matthew 5:39) suggests to not respond to violence with further violence, as this would worsen the situation. Its core meaning is that an evil person can only be overcome by goodness. Why? Because it preserves the peace of the individual incurring the slap, thus allowing them to keep free from anger and its destructiveness. It teaches us to preference peace and forbearance over violent acts. It should be noted that such teachings set forth do not contradict the state's need and right to protect its citizens and to punish criminals. They rather addresses our actions and responsibilities as individuals.

What further reinforces what was said above is the teaching of Christ that, *"Blessed be the peacemakers, for they shall be called the sons of God"* (Matthew 5:9). Peace brings us as Christian individuals into communion with God to the extent of being called His sons and daughters. Peace also brings us into harmony with the world God created. It is in essence the imitation of the Lord Christ and

> ONLY THE PEACE of God assures us all that we are not alone

Fruits of the Life with God

therefore only peacemakers can share in God's peace, share it with others, and participate in the work of Christ as the King of Peace. If we do so, we become one with the Lord Jesus Christ.

Only the peace of God keeps fear in check. Only the peace of God assures us all that we are not alone regardless of what is happening in the world, in our communities, and in our workplaces. Peace gives us the presence of God working in our lives, making us confident that whatever comes our way can be taken care of. St. Paul teaches concerning this, *"And we know that all things work together for good to those who love God, to those who are the called according to His purpose"* (Romans 8:28).

The pursuit of peace be to all.

Love

These was a blessed woman named Ruth whose mother in law, Naomi, suffered the loss of her husband and two sons. The following are the words spoken by Ruth to her after this occurred,

> *"Entreat me not to leave you, or to turn back from following after you; for wherever you go, I will go; and wherever you lodge, I will lodge; your people shall be my people, and your God, my God. Where you die, I will die, and there will I be buried. The Lord do so to me, and*

> *more also, if anything but death parts you and me"* (Ruth 1:16-17)

What a great display of selfless love! The question posed though is, can I really love someone who isn't my own flesh and blood? Many have to answer this question whether contemplating a close or spiritual friendship, marriage, interacting with prospective in-laws or perhaps even the adoption of someone into a family unit. On another level, this question also relates to those serving within the church and how they ought to love those whom they serve.

It should be contemplated and prayed about regardless of the service, whether it be serving sandwiches, cleaning the church and bathrooms, teaching in Sunday School or anything else.

Service should never be a set of chores or a task list. It is also not something to be carried out at a particular time once a week.

Serving the church is about much more than showing up when others do not, or counting the number of years spent in service to the Church. So what should service look like? We read that, *"God is love, and those who abide in love abide in God and God abides in them"* (1 John 4:16). This is the foundation of service. It should be a spring of life to those who are served and a reflection of the servant's love for God.

The beginning of service first involves realising the limitless and boundless love God gives to us, epitomised by the verse,

> *"God so loved the world that He gave His only Son, so that everyone who believes in Him may not perish but may have eternal life"* (John 3:16)

Once we are filled with His love towards us, we are naturally able to offer all our hearts to Him in return.

As one's love for God abundantly increases, one is then led to the path of loving and serving others. A conversation between Christ and St. Peter highlights this,

> *"When they had finished breakfast, Jesus said to Simon Peter, 'Simon son of John, do you love Me more than these?' He said to Him, 'Yes, Lord; You know that I love You.' The Lord Jesus Christ said to him, 'Feed My lambs'"* (John 21:15)

Note that St. Peter was only asked to feed His lambs after first answering the question, *"do you love Me?"*

Service should always ask of itself, "Is my service what it should be?"

How much effort a servant puts in, the extent of their striving, is actually the aspect of the service that shows the servant cares and is performing the service wholeheartedly. Striving is visiting the sick at home and in the hospital. It is sitting with someone who has lost a loved one. It is reading the Holy Bible to the elderly who have poor vision. Striving is providing transportation to church services to those who have none. It is calling students to enquire if they need anything while away at college. It is the giving of the message, "I care."

We need to stop and ask ourselves if our service to God is full of this love or if it is as barren and dry as a desert. Do we feel that we display love and care to those whom we serve, the same way we wished our servants to have cared about us? Words like, "I'm too busy" or "there isn't enough time" indicate that one's love for their service is weak.

Do we actually need to care about the children we serve at church even beyond that context and on days other than Sunday? Consider what King Solomon writes, *"Two are better than one, because they have a good reward for their labour. For if they fall, one will lift up his companion. But woe to him who is alone when he falls, for he has no one to help him up"* (Ecclesiastes 4:9-10). Have we considered the meaning of this verse in relation to those we serve, rather than the meaning it may have for us alone?

Fruits of the Life with God

Can it be said about us as the servants providing a service, "I look up to my servant, they are a guiding star, they taught me a lot, they are a candle burning brightly, they provide a listening ear to me and are concerned about my spiritual welfare"?

Just as the sun is the servant of the earth and its heat allows the earth to be productive, a servant should similarly be the same in relation to those they serve. In turn like the trees and flowers, abundant fruits are formed in those who are served. This essence of service in turn leads us to the Eternal Spirit that is truly fruitful, bearing the fullness of love.

> *THIS ESSENCE OF service in turn leads us to the Eternal Spirit that is truly fruitful, bearing the fullness of love*

Let us all pray that where we are, there is love of service to God. May it be a love exhibited by a fruitful sweetness that can only be tasted through affection, kindness and support. May we serve in order to give of ourselves to others, and not so that we can gain praise for it. Christ says,

> *"I give you a new commandment, that you love one another. Just as I have loved you, you should also love one another"* (John 13:34)

Therefore may we love as He loves and put all our hearts into His service.

Joy

Joy is an integral part of a harmonious life lived out for the glory of God and our personal fulfilment. Nowadays, one of the most common problems is the lack of joy, especially among young people. They are constantly bombarded with pressures and stresses concerning various aspects of their lives. If the ones serving God do not themselves have joy then it will be difficult for them to relay that joy to those around them. To say we experience joy is to be able to live joyfully even during the most difficult situations; not only so, but to be able to communicate it biblically, psychologically and traditionally to those whom we serve.

Independent of personality, circumstances, maturity level, or exposure, we have all been created "in [God's] image, according to [His] likeness" (Genesis 1:26). There is a difference between God's image and His likeness though. The former is what we have been created in; the latter is what we have the potential to develop into. The term "likeness" denotes the fulfilment and realisation which we aspire for through spiritual and psychological growth. Actualising and fulfilling this image is what St. Paul described as "till we all come to the unity of the faith and of the knowledge of the Son of God, to a perfect man, to the measure of the stature of the fullness of Christ" (Ephesians 4:13). That is, that we reach the likeness of Jesus, which is our ultimate goal.

Sensing, intuition, thinking, and feeling are the four aspects of a human personality. God has the four aspects completely developed in Him. When we wholly develop these four aspects in us, we become Christ-like, in the likeness of God. Each of the four gospels is said to demonstrate an aspect of the personality of Jesus Christ, with Matthew, Mark, Luke and John reflecting the thinking, sensing, feeling and intuition aspects, respectively.

Inward joy, one of the characteristics of a Christian, is the manifestation of someone who is well-developed in the feeling aspect of their personality. Being joyful is not dependent on circumstances, because no matter what happens, a true Christian should be radiant and capable of illuminating their surroundings. This is because a true Christian who keeps Heaven in mind will remain serene and cheerful even on the darkest of days. They do so by drawing support from the deep river of joy that the Holy Spirit has set course for within them.

Some of the other characteristics of someone who is well-developed in the feeling aspect of their personality include,

Loyalty and Fidelity

❖ Just as God is love, so He is faithful also. Our unfaithfulness does not cancel nor alter God's as St. Paul says, "For what if some did not believe? Will their unbelief make the faithfulness of God without effect? Certainly not" (Romans 3:3-4). In order for us to develop into the likeness of Christ, we have to practise faithfulness and loyalty. It says, "Dwell in the land, and feed on His faithfulness" (Psalm 37:3). Our faithfulness to God and to others should remain constant even when they are not.

Doing God's will

❖ The joy of Christ, who being equal to the Father, consisted in doing His Father's will. He told us, "My food is to do the will of Him who sent Me, and to finish His work" (John 4:34). This was so important in His life, that it was even more satisfying than the necessity of food. Joy came out of serving and pleasing the heavenly Father. It was a common recurring theme of His life and ministry.

Means of nourishing and developing the feeling aspect within us, which in turn nourishes our inner joy, are as follows,

Remembering

- ❖ Remembering and sharing good news with others is a sure source of happiness. David the Psalmist expressed this truth in Psalm 133:1, "Behold, how good and how pleasant it is for brethren to dwell together in unity." The act of remembering happy occasions, moments, and incidents brings about joy in the heart. That is the aim behind celebrating feasts, anniversaries, and recalling happy events. Positive memories energise feelings, heal wounds, and deepen commitments to the covenants that bind us. In the same way, commemorating major events like the Nativity, Resurrection and celebrating feasts of the saints, all renew our commitments to God and open us up for hope, healing, and renewal of life. This joy-generating concept of celebrating and sharing the good news is found in many of Christ's parables. For example, in that of the lost son in Luke 15, his return to his father is followed by a grand celebration. Concerning the parable Christ says, "there will be more joy in heaven over one sinner who repents" (Luke 15:7). This parable gives us insight into the heart of God which is willing to celebrate and share His pure joy, especially that of the return of the lost.

Repeating

- In the book of Deuteronomy 4:9-10, God commands Moses, his children, and his children's children to remember how He, the Almighty, had rescued the Israelites from the land of Egypt delivering them with a mighty hand. This positively confirms the importance of Tradition in our spiritual and social practices. Tradition is the retelling of an old story over and over again. In doing so, we nourish our present and protect our future. The outcome of these commemorating experiences is an emotion called gratitude. The term is derived from the root word "grace". So, gratitude is a joyful reaction to the graces obtained. Whoever forgets the graces of God will never be grateful and consequently will never experience joy. There is an inevitable link between the three elements: prayer, joy, and thanksgiving. They are commands issued from God directly for us to obey and implement, "Rejoice always, pray without ceasing, in everything give thanks; for this is the will of God in Christ Jesus for you" (1 Thessalonians 5:16-17). The links in the chain are interrelated and interdependent; so much so that a breakdown in one will lead to a breakdown in the cycle; since each one feeds off the other. David has fulfilled this command expressively in Psalm 103:1-5, praying, rejoicing, and giving thanks while remembering the good deeds that God has done to him; *"Bless the Lord, O my soul; and all that is within me, bless His holy name! Bless the Lord, O my soul, And forget not all His benefits: Who forgives all your iniquities, Who heals all your diseases, Who redeems your life from destruction, Who crowns you with loving-kindness and tender mercies, Who satisfies your mouth with good things"*

In the same psalm mentioned above, David is prophetically being reminded by the Holy Spirit of the real source of all these benefits that he is surrounded with. That being the redemptive act of our Lord Jesus Christ on the cross. Without this redemption, we would still be in bondage reaping the fruits of pain, death, and destruction. *"For as the heavens are high above the earth, So great is His mercy toward those who fear Him; As far as the east is from the west, So far has He removed our transgressions from us. As a father pities his children, so the Lord pities those who fear Him. For He knows our frame; He remembers that we are dust"* (Psalm 103:11-14). Christ pitied us and came to die on the cross for our sake to offer us salvation.

There are then causes for a lack of joy which include,

Sin

- ❖ The centre of feelings is the heart. Much evidence from the Holy Bible proves sin to be the main cause of hardness of heart including Psalm 106 and Isaiah 1:4. Thus, a hardened heart due to sin cannot experience the gift of joy. In opposition to the productive positive cycle that exists in a joyful heart, a negative one emerges in a hardened heart. This is because sin leads to hardness of heart and hardness of heart leads to lack of joy. Unless the source of sin is eliminated, this cycle will not be replaced with the one which has praise, gratitude and joy as its components. Hardness of heart is considered a spiritual amnesia, a spiritual psychological condition in which we experience forgetfulness of God's grace and goodness and dwell in our negative thoughts and self-centeredness. God warns against this perilous state of mind and heart in Deuteronomy 8:11, "Beware that you do not forget the Lord your God by not keeping His commandments, His judgments, and His statutes which I command you today."

Lack of Commemoration

❖ When people stop commemorating significant incidents in their lives in which God's love and care was manifested to them, they may stop offering thanksgiving, and this eventually leads to absence of joy.

Loss of Focus

❖ When one begins to focus on the wrong things in life and prioritises them, they lose sight of what is important. That is, they begin to forget that their relationship with God is the source of maintaining joy and living the joyful life. They thus miss what joy is all about.

The consequences of the absence of joy are manifold, of which some are explained below,

Loss of Power

❖ A powerful verse that highlights this says, "For the joy of the Lord is your strength" (Nehemiah 8:10). Therefore, according to this biblical truth, lack of joy equals lack of strength. A sad heart cannot have a strong positive outlook on life nor to all that is in it. This condition will then reflect on the person's spiritual life and how they perceive church rituals and practices. For example, an unhappy heart will not enjoy the treasures existing in the Divine Liturgy. The Divine Liturgy is essentially a reliving of the redemptive act of Christ, regarding which He says, "Do this in remembrance of Me" (Luke 22:19). Having missed the mark, they will experience frustration and impatience and their worship will consequently turn into a lifeless one. God described this psychological emotional state, also experienced by the Israelites, saying "These people draw near to Me with their mouth, and honour Me with their lips, but their heart is far from Me" (Matthew 15:8). Contrary to such an apathetical state of mind and attitude is the priest's joyful one. In concluding the Liturgy rituals, the serving priest concludes by saying "our mouth is filled with joy and our tongue with gladness." Such joy is available to all members of the congregation.

Loss of Faithfulness

❖ A sad heart becomes unfaithful to God, and thus alienates itself from Him, the very source of its life and talents. St. Paul speaks extensively of this state of denial of the source of all things and the subsequent pretentious thinking when he writes, "And what do you have that you did not receive? Now if you did indeed receive it, why do you boast as if you had not received it?" (1 Corinthians 4:7). As a result of this mental and emotional apathy, joy gets replaced with sadness, depression and loss of spiritual vision.

It begs the question, how then can joy be recovered? The following are only a few tools,

Holy Contrition

❖ Sadness and grief can be made use of in a beneficial way. They can be altered in nature and turned into a holy one leading to repentance and change. Such grief will then gain a new name and be described as holy, thus leading to full joy. As it is written, "For godly sorrow produces repentance leading to salvation, not to be regretted" (2 Corinthians 7:10). A very prominent character who experienced this double fold process is the prodigal son (in a parable Christ taught in Luke 15) who, all of a sudden, awoke from his spiritual amnesia and desired to return to his father. He recalled his father's mercy, grace, love, and acceptance and therefore possessed true contrition that led to repentance (the parable symbolising our interaction with God, we being the prodigal son and God being the father). This transformation of grief into joy and sorrow into compassion comes from one place and one place only; that being the redemptive act of Jesus Christ on the cross. Those who have not entered the experience of God's free merciful act on the cross cannot be disposed to accept compassion from others nor show it to them. We need God's redemptive mercy to be activated and actualised in our lives before we can manifest and bestow it on others.

Shift in Focus

❖ When we start to focus on the right thing, that being our relationship with God, only then will we be able to relax and rejoice and sing with St. Paul, "who shall separate us from the love of Christ?" (Romans 8:35). This is a learning process which even St. Paul had to go through himself before he could say "I have learned" (Philippians 4:11), referring to learning the secret of being joyful and content in any and every situation. David the Psalmist had his focus and priorities rightfully established, and that is what led him to experience an everlasting joy, as he says, "I have set the LORD always before me; because He is at my right hand I shall not be moved" (Psalm 16:8).

Here comes the role of the Holy Spirit as an Intercessor, Teacher, and Comforter. There is a prayer called the Litany for the Sick which is prayed by the priest, requesting psychological and physical healing addresses seven needs. Those being mercy, rest, refreshment, grace, help, salvation, and forgiveness. Thus when we call upon God, we find that the exclusive tenderness of Jesus Christ heals from all kinds of injuries including physical, psychological, and emotional injuries. He is truly the Helper of the helpless, the Hope of the hopeless, the Comfort of the faint-hearted and the source of all joy.

The joy of the Lord is the answer to living a meaningful life, and the one very important element in completing the character of a Christian. Joy gives us a taste of what heaven must be like. So much so, that even when life strips us of all the circumstances that would normally bring a sense of happiness, we will be able to boldly profess that, "though the fig tree may not blossom, nor fruit be on the vines; though the labor of the olive may fail, And the fields yield no food; though the flock may be cut off from the fold, and there be no herd in the stalls. Yet I will rejoice in the Lord, I will joy in the God of my salvation" (Habakkuk 3:17-18).

Self-Control

It is written, *"A man without self-control is like a city broken into and left without walls"* (Proverbs 25:28).

This description shows how important self-control is, since it acts as a guard to our life. As the verse says, a man without self-control is like a city broken into and left without protection, easy for thieves to break into, steal and destroy. Likewise, if we leave our soul and spirit without self-control, the devil can easily enter and spoil our lives. Self-control is therefore important for everyone without exception regardless of gender, age or position.

Self-Control in its essence is dominance over all desires. It is one of the most important spiritual virtues that are essential for growth in the knowledge of God, pursuit of the Truth, and attaining of our future destiny.

As human beings, our flesh is driven by its physical desires such as the desire for food and sex, or psychological desires such as the love of fame and praise, to name a few. St. Paul describes the body's desire to obtain and maintain these things as an ongoing war between the flesh and the spirit, since the spirit also has its desire to obtain what is beyond food and fame. When we allow our desires to control us, we become similar to animals, which are driven by their instinctive desires with neither dominance nor control. On the other hand, when we subject our flesh with all its desires to the leadership of the spirit, we exercise what we call self-control, which differentiates us human beings from animals.

Self-control is not attainable in isolation from other important basic Christian fundamentals. Like links in a chain, St. Peter expresses this interdependence and interrelation of virtues in 2 Peter 1:5-7, "But also for this very reason, giving all diligence, add to your faith virtue, to virtue knowledge, to knowledge self-control, to self-control perseverance to perseverance godliness, to godliness brotherly kindness, and to brotherly kindness love."

Let us follow this chain of virtues and understand the links between them, keeping in mind their order in the above verses.

Faith

- ❖ Which is supported by virtue. We read regarding faith that it is, "the substance of things hoped for, the evidence of things not seen" (Hebrews 11:1). God has promised us great things among which are eternal life with Him and partaking in His Divine Nature. We, through faith, look forward to the fulfilment of these promises; and while doing so, we support our faith with virtue and good deeds. This being so for, "faith without works is dead" (James 2:26).

Virtue

- ❖ Which is supported by knowledge. This knowledge comprises the capacity to discern between good and bad and between right and wrong. Such discernment is achieved only through knowledge of the Holy Scriptures, as the Psalm says, "Your word is a lamp to my feet" (Psalm 119:105).

Knowledge

- ❖ Which is reinforced by self-control. Self-control, the focus of this section, is necessary for the Word of God to become real and applicable in our life.

Self-control

❖ Which is maintained by perseverance. Christ mentions in the gospel that, "He who endures to the end will be saved" (Mark 13:13). These are our Lord's words concerning the significance of perseverance in salvation. In order for one to control themselves and have dominance over their desires, one needs to practice patience and endurance, without which self-control will avail nothing.

Perseverance

❖ Which is braced by godliness. Suffering and hardships can never be endured without the aspiration for godliness. Why does a student endure the long hours of studying except for the desire of success? Likewise it is for the sake of godliness that we persevere in our pursuit of self-control, which in turn strengthens the above mentioned virtues in the chain. Mistaken are those who think of godliness as an austere extreme style of living that does not befit their lives in this day and age. Such people are cheating themselves and will end up in great sorrow. Solomon in the book of Wisdom, chapter 8 verse 7 says, "And if anyone loves righteousness, her labors are virtues; for she teaches self-control and prudence, justice and courage; nothing in life is more profitable for mortals than these." Love of righteousness will develop virtue in us which in turn will help us acquire prudence, justice, and courage. Nothing in life is more profitable to humanity than these qualities.

Godliness

❖ Which is followed by brotherly kindness. According to Ecclesiastes 4:9, "Two are better than one." Fellowship in prayer, Bible study and other church activities and examples of brotherly kindness will support our godly life.

Brotherly Kindness

❖ Which is supported by love, that is, love for God and for one another. St. John states it clearly that we cannot claim to love God whom we do not see if we do not love our brother whom we see.

The martyrs offered their lives on the altar of love for Christ. In these modern days, the chance for us to offer on the same alter exists, not by giving up our lives but by sacrificing the desires for an easy luxurious life. When teaching their children self-control, parents should start teaching them how to love God and enter into a personal relationship with

Christ before they can take leadership over their desires. St. Paul says,

> *"But what things were gain to me, these I have counted loss for Christ. Yet indeed I also count all things loss for the excellence of the knowledge of Christ Jesus my Lord, for whom I have suffered the loss of all things, and count them as rubbish, that I may gain Christ and be found in Him"* (Philippians 3:7-9)

He did not care about what he had lost because he knew he had gained what is more precious and everlasting, that being Christ. It is the love of God which supports brotherly kindness, which in turn reinforces godliness, which then strengthens perseverance, thereby sustaining self-control, which itself is needed for knowledge, thus providing for virtue, which finally feeds into faith.

St. Peter writes,

> *"As His divine power has given to us all things that pertain to life and godliness, through the knowledge of Him who called us by glory and virtue, by which have been given to us exceedingly great and precious promises, that through these you may be partakers of the divine nature, having escaped the corruption that is in the world through lust"* (2 Peter 1:3-4)

Fruits of the Life with God

That is how he sums up the reason for developing self-control. The cause of corruption comes from within us because of our earthly desires. However, the cure from it lies in the love that we develop for God. We can then say that the biggest motivation to exercise self-control, which is not an easy task, is mainly love for God. If we really love God from all our heart, we will be ready to sacrifice all desires. An instance of sacrificing life for the love of God is what the martyrs did and are still doing following the example of St. Paul who professed, *"nor do I count my life dear to myself, so that I may finish my race with joy, and the ministry which I received from the Lord Jesus, to testify to the gospel of the grace of God"* (Acts 20:24).

The best analogy that well describes the spiritual marathon of a Christian is what again St. Paul offers in 1 Corinthians 9, comparing a believer to an athlete who in his desire to win a race sets before his eyes a clear goal, that being winning the race. To achieve that, he monitors all his steps including the quantity of food, amount of sleep and level of exercise. While an athlete does it for a perishable crown, we as Christians have our spiritual goal for an imperishable crown.

> *"Do you not know that those who run in a race all run, but one receives the prize? Run in such a way that you may obtain it. And everyone who competes for the prize is temperate in all*

things. Now they do it to obtain a perishable crown, but we for an imperishable crown" (1 Corinthians 9:24-25)

Self-control is clearly a prerequisite for winning that imperishable crown lest we become disqualified.

How then are we ought to develop self-control? There are some points to be considered,

Submit to the Holy Spirit

❖ In order to develop the fruit of self-control, we must resort to its ultimate source, that is, the Holy Spirit. Therefore, obtaining the former entails submission to the latter. When we submit our flesh to the spirit and our spirit to God, we will have set foot on the path to self-control. Hence, the Holy Spirit will have leadership over our life and His fruit and actions will become mine. That is why it is essential to let the Holy Spirit control every aspect of our lives in order that He may direct our minds and actions, thereby transforming us into the likeness of Christ. Double mindedness or half submission of our lives will only grieve the Holy Spirit and quench His work in us and thus will not lead to the development of self-control in us.

❖ Develop the chain of virtues

❖ In the chain of the eight prerequisites mentioned earlier in 2 Peter 1:5-7, self-control falls predominantly at the centre, thereby acting as a pivot point for all the other Christian fundamentals. This is because our faith will not be manifested without virtue, which in turn will require faith to stand before all challenges and adversities. In order to exercise virtue, we need knowledge and appreciation of God's word and His will in our lives. This knowledge is only attainable through the exercising and practising of self-control over our senses, habits and desires. However, self-control takes time and effort which is why it is supported by perseverance. This perseverance however, should by no means be mere stoical endurance, but flowing from and supported by God Himself. Once God supports us, we will be in a position to achieve godliness. Then having set foot on the road to godliness, brotherly kindness will be a by-product of it and an offspring of the love of God. Such love being poured into our hearts by the Holy Spirit, as it pronounces, *"because the love of God has been poured out in our hearts by the Holy Spirit who was given to us"* (Romans 5:5).

Thus, the chain of Christian fundamentals has no end and no beginning; for it ends where it has seemingly started and starts where it has seemingly ended with no definite end nor definite beginning.

Faith ⟷ Virtue ⟷ Knowledge ⟷ Self Control ⟷Perseverance ⟷ Godliness ⟷ Brotherly Kindness ⟷ Love.

Acquire Spiritual Friendship

- ❖ Spiritual friendship has its roots in brotherly kindness. When we surround ourselves with friends who have spiritual maturity, they become a source of support and enhancement for our own spiritual growth. Married couples can become spiritual friends to each other so that any time any of the two weakens or falls away, the other member will help restore their partner. Those who are not married can still have spiritual friends with whom they may hold prayer and fellowship meetings and so support each other emotionally and spiritually. St. Paul stresses the significance of spiritual friendship in Galatians 6 where he says, "Brethren, if a man is overtaken in any trespass, you who are spiritual restore such a one in a spirit of gentleness" (Galatians 6:1). He requires that we do not neglect the importance of vigilance over oneself in the process though, "considering yourself lest you also be tempted" (Galatians 6:1).

Set a Clear Goal

❖ Any successful endeavour is unequivocally preceded by a clear goal. Our Lord Jesus Christ had a clear goal before Him, which was our salvation. The clarity of the goal thus facilitated the means (the Cross) and procured the joyful end result expressed in His words of triumphant accomplishment: "It is finished" (John 19:30). Likewise, St. Paul had his goal clear before him: "For to me, to live is Christ, and to die is gain" (Philippians 1:21). Not wasting his time aimlessly, and eliminating any impeding factors, he declared, "Therefore I run thus: not with uncertainty. Thus I fight: not as one who beats the air" (1 Corinthians 9:26), until he could boldly and successfully say: "Finally, there is laid up for me the crown of righteousness" (2 Timothy 4:8).

In addition to all that was mentioned above, there are also particular spiritual practices that play a pivotal role in the development of self-control and disciplining the body. It is written, "But I discipline my body and bring it into subjection, lest, when I have preached to others, I myself should become disqualified" (1 Corinthians 9:27). How did St. Paul set about doing that? He definitely did so by exhibiting the following,

Fasting

- ❖ A very beneficial exercise and powerful tool for developing self-control. Fasting is the ability to say "no" to the desire for food. This ability will eventually develop self-control and strengthen the will to say "no" to sin. Our Lord instituted fasting by practicing it Himself. The need for fasting is equivalent to the need for self-control. God does not benefit from our fasting, nor is it a law to fast. It is us who benefit from fasting. Fasting should also be carried out in the proper way and not according to our convenience. When we fast according to our own rules, we are exhibiting lack of self-control.

Three important cornerstones of fasting are:

- ❖ Abstaining for some time (at least till noon or according to our spiritual father's direction)
- ❖ Controlling the quantity of food
- ❖ Monitoring the quality of food

Establishing these three foundations of fasting will surely lead to discipline, which is in essence the core of self-control. There are exemptions from fasting, however, for the sick, elderly or those who physically cannot do so. This should be discussed with their spiritual father.

Abstention from sexual pleasures

❖ St. Paul urged married people not to indulge in their marital relations during the church fasting periods in order that the couple may dedicate themselves to worship. However, he implored that abstention from marital relationship should only be done under two conditions, being that it is by agreement on both sides and only for a limited time. The reason for these two conditions is to not allow the devil to tempt either side because of lack of self-control.

"Do not deprive one another except with consent for a time, that you may give yourselves to fasting and prayer; and come together again so that Satan does not tempt you because of your lack of self-control" (1 Corinthians 7:5)

Prostration

❖ Which may appear as merely an exercise of physically disciplining the body, yet is in fact an important spiritual practice. "Come let us kneel" are the words by which we start the Morning Hour Prayers. Unfortunately, prostration has gradually disappeared from many people's worship. Nonetheless, bowing and kneeling to the ground is essential to practise lowliness and subjection to the Holy Spirit. Prostrating, either at the beginning of or in the midst of prayer saying, "God have mercy on me, I am a sinner" at least ten times (or according to the spiritual father's direction) is a good practice. A lot of blessings, including the fruit of self-control, come from prostration before God.

Body posture in prayer

- ❖ "Teach us how to stand before You at the time of prayer and offer you befitting glorification" is what we ask God when we are about to pray the Prayers of Praise (also called the Midnight Prayer). Standing upright in a respectful manner is required while praying. It shows reverence and respect to the One we are praying to, following what the Bible says, "I desire therefore that the men pray everywhere, lifting up holy hands, without wrath and doubting" (1 Timothy 2:8).

Serving others

- ❖ *"If anyone desires to be first, he shall be last of all and servant of all"* (Mark 9:35). This is our Lord's precept concerning true greatness. Serving others helps reduce our self-conceit, love of praise, and selfishness. We never read in the Holy Bible about our Lord being served. He said, "For even the Son of Man did not come to be served, but to serve" (Mark 10:45). Whoever wants to be Christ-like has to follow

His footsteps, imitate His lifestyle and adopt His mission. Whenever it becomes difficult, we need to remind ourselves of the reality that "without Me you can do nothing" (John 15:5).

Thus is the importance and place of self-control in the life of a Christian who has his clear goal in life, wants to get to know and be liberated by the Truth and looks at this life as a journey that prepares for the everlasting life. Such a person will always seek to control his mind, thoughts and senses knowing that, "A man without self-control is like a city broken into and left without walls" (Proverbs 25:28).

The Beatitudes

In the Gospel writings, the beatitudes introduce the teachings of Jesus and are traditionally considered to contain the most concise summary of the spiritual life of man. Thus, it is the clear teaching of the Gospel and the Church that one enters into the mysteries of Christ and the Kingdom of God only by way of following the Lord's teachings in the beatitudes.

> *"And He opened His mouth and taught them, saying:*
>
> *'Blessed are the poor in spirit, for theirs is the kingdom of heaven.*
>
> *Blessed are those who mourn, for they shall be comforted.*
>
> *Blessed are the meek, for they shall inherit the earth.*
>
> *Blessed are those who hunger and thirst for*

righteousness, for they shall be filled.

Blessed are the merciful, for they shall obtain mercy.

Blessed are the pure in heart, for they shall see God.

Blessed are the peacemakers, for they shall be called sons of God.

Blessed are those who are persecuted for righteousness sake, for theirs is the kingdom of heaven.

Blessed are you when they revile and persecute you, and say all kinds of evil against you falsely for My sake.

Rejoice and be exceedingly glad, for great is your reward in heaven.'"

(Mt 5.2–12; cf. Lk 6.20–26)

Each of the beatitudes will be discussed below.

Poverty in Spirit

"Blessed are the poor in spirit, for theirs is the kingdom of heaven" (Matthew 5:3)

This first beatitude is the fundamental condition for all man's spiritual progress and growth. Before everything else, if a person wants to live a life with God, he must be poor in spirit.

To be poor in spirit is to recognise clearly that we have nothing which we have not received from God and that we are nothing without the grace of God. This poverty is called "spiritual" in St. Matthew's Gospel because it is primarily an attitude of mind and a conviction of the soul. It is the condition of man in total emptiness and openness before God.

To be poor in spirit is to be devoid of all pride and trust in one's own power. It is to be freed from all reliance on one's own ideas, opinions and desires. Moreover, it is to be liberated from the *"vain imaginations of one's own heart"* (Jeremiah 23:17, Romans 1:21). The holy Virgin Saint Mary, the perfect model of poverty in spirit, sang concerning this matter in her magnificent praise,

> *"God has shown strength with His arm, He has scattered the proud in the imagination of their hearts, He has put down the mighty from their thrones, And has exalted the humble and meek, He has filled the hungry with good things, And the rich He has sent away empty"* (Luke 1:51–54)

Jesus Himself was poor, not only in worldly possessions but also in spirit. He had "no place to lay His head" (Matthew 8:20) indeed, but such physical poverty was the direct result of His perfect poverty in spirit.

If a person wishes to embark on the spiritual life, he must abandon all things and follow Christ in poverty of spirit. To be poor in spirit is simply to be wholly set free from the sinful lusts of this world.

> "If anyone loves this world, love for the Father is not in him. For all that is in the world, the lust of the eyes and the pride of life, is not of the Father, but is of the world. And the world passes away, and the lust of it; but he who does the will of God abides forever" (1 John 2:15–17)

> *If a person wishes to embark on the spiritual life, he must abandon all things and follow Christ in poverty of spirit*

The first revelation of the will of God is that His children be poor in spirit. The violation of this spiritual attitude is the original sin and the source of all sorrows.

Blessed Mourning

> *"Blessed are those who mourn, for they shall be comforted"* (Matthew 5:4)

This is the second beatitude, and it logically follows the first. If one is poor in spirit, liberated from the physical lusts of this world, he will necessarily mourn and weep over the condition of man.

The poor in spirit knows how foolish and sad it is to be caught by sin and its deceitfulness and to be wedded to death. When the poor in spirit views the reality of this world, that its riches and attractions are all vain and meaningless, they cannot help but mourn for the "wretched, pitiable, poor, blind and naked" state of those people who chase these things (Revelations 3:17). Knowing the sublimity of life with God in comparison causes the spiritually poor person to mourn and weep for those who are ignorant of it. They become likened to the prophets who mourned over the corruption of Israel and like Jesus Himself when He wept over the corpse of Lazarus and the sins of the city of Jerusalem (John 11:35, Matthew 23:37).

Blessed mourning for sin is essential to the spiritual life. What differentiates it from worldly mourning, however, is that it is not morbid or joyless. It stems from the victory of Christ and so it is in fact filled with hope, gladness and light.

St. Paul also comments on this type of blessed mourning when he writes, *"For godly grief produces a repentance that leads to salvation and brings no regret, but worldly grief produces death. For see what earnestness this godly grief has produced in you"* (2 Corinthians 7:9–11).

St. John Climacus, one of the 7th century fathers of the church, writes concerning this that it is a "mourning which causes joy". Indeed the outcome of blessed mourning is not despondency or remorse, but rather repentance and salvation. He writes further,

> *"Mourning, according to God, is sadness of soul and the disposition of a sorrowing heart which ever madly seeks for that which it thirsts ...*
>
> *Mourning is a golden spur in a soul which is stripped of all attachment and all ties ...*
>
> *Keep a firm hold of the blessed joy-grief of holy mourning and do not stop working at it until it raises you high above the things of this world and presents you pure to Christ"*
>
> (The Ladder of Divine Ascent, Step 7)

Truly blessed are those who mourn for their sins and of those around them, for God will surely comfort them.

Meekness

> *"Blessed are the meek, for they shall inherit the earth"* (Matthew 5:5)

Meekness is another essential possession of the spiritual person. Jesus Himself was meek, choosing to focus on this virtue in particular when asking us to emulate Him. He says,

> *"Come to Me, all who labor and are heavy laden, and I will give you rest. Take My yoke upon you and learn from Me; for I am meek and lowly in heart, and you will find rest for your souls"* (Matthew 11:27–30)

The apostles of Christ also taught meekness, including Saints James and Paul, who both insist upon it.

St James writes,

> *"Who is wise and understanding among you? By his good life let him show his works in the meekness of wisdom. But if you have bitter jealousy and selfish ambition in your hearts, do not boast and be false to the truth. This wisdom is not such as it comes down from above, but is earthly, unspiritual, devilish. For where jealousy and selfish ambition exist, there will be disorder and every vile practice. But the wisdom from above is first pure, then peaceable, gentle, open to reason, full of mercy and good fruits"* (James 3:13–17)

To be meek means to be gentle and kind and empty of all selfishness. In other words, a meek person never returns evil for evil, but always overcomes evil by good. That is, meekness means to reject every thought and action of violence, which in any case can never produce fruitful results.

Having a firm conviction that doing good is more powerful than evil is another feature of a meek person.

To refer once more to St. John Climacus,

> *Meekness is an unchangeable state of mind which remains the same in honour and dishonour. Meekness is the rock overlooking the sea of irritability which breaks all the waves that dash against it, remaining itself unmoved. Meekness is the buttress of patience, the mother of love and the foundation of wisdom, for it is said, "The Lord will teach the meek His way" (Psalm 24:9) ... In meek hearts the Lord finds rest, but a turbulent soul is the seat of the devil.*

(The Ladder of Divine Ascent, Step 24)

Hunger and Thirst for Righteousness

> *"Blessed are they who hunger and thirst for righteousness, for they shall be filled" (Matthew 5:6).*

Strictly speaking, this beatitude of the Lord blesses, not the righteous, but the seekers of righteousness.

It is those who are hungry and thirsty for what is good who receive the blessings of God. Christ also says,

> "Therefore do not worry, saying, 'What shall we eat?' or 'What shall we drink?' or 'What shall we wear?' For after all these things the Gentiles seek. For your heavenly Father knows that you need all these things. But seek first the kingdom of God and His righteousness, and all these things shall be added to you" (Matthew 6:31–33)

Man's life consists of seeking, hungering and thirsting for righteousness. This is the spiritual teaching of the scriptures and the saints. The satisfaction and rest come from God, and yet are themselves the basis of further hunger and thirst. This may seem as a contradiction to Christ's teaching that, *"he who comes to Me shall not hunger, and he who believes in Me shall never thirst"* (John 6:35). However, this is not the case as it is rather the affirmation that man's heart, as St. Augustine (5th c.) said, is created "toward God," and that the "rest" which is found in Him is itself an "ever-dynamic rest," as stated by St. Maximus (7th c.). Thus, the rest that comes from God is always growing in ever greater union with the uncontainable and inexhaustible richness of divine life.

St. Gregory of Nyssa (4th c.) said it this way,

> *"It is impossible for our human nature ever to stop moving; it has been made of its Creator ever to keep changing. Hence when we prevent it from using its energy on trifles and keep it on all sides from doing what it should not, it must necessarily move in a straight path towards truth."*

This spiritual teaching means that the truly spiritual person will not merely move from unrighteousness to righteousness, but will continue to grow to an ever-greater righteousness and perfection in God. The spiritual hunger and thirst in this way is an essential characteristic of a righteous person. Moreover, the apostle Paul gave the following doctrine,

> *"But one thing I do, forgetting what lies behind, and straining forward to what lies ahead, I press on toward the goal for the prize of the upward call of God in Christ Jesus." (Philippians 3:13–16). Hence there is no satisfaction for man's spirit but God and it is one of continuous progression in union with Him.*

To hunger and thirst for God, "for the living God" (Psalm 42:2) is spiritual life. To be filled and satisfied with anything else is death for the soul.

Mercy

"Blessed are the merciful, for they shall obtain mercy" (Matthew 5:7)

To be merciful is to be like God for, "The Lord is merciful and gracious, slow to anger and abounding in steadfast love" (Psalm 103:8).

Elsewhere He is described as, "The Lord, the Lord, a God merciful and gracious, slow to anger and abounding in steadfast love for thousands, forgiving iniquity and transgression and sin" (Exodus 34:6–7). Additionally, this is also the teaching of Christ in His Sermon on the Mountain,

"Love your enemies and do good and lend, expecting nothing in return; and your reward will be great, and you will be children of the Most High; for He is kind to the ungrateful and the selfish. Be merciful, even as your Father is merciful
(Luke 6:35–36)

To be merciful does not mean to justify sin. It does not mean to be tolerant of foolishness and evil. It also does not mean to overlook injustice.

To be merciful means to have compassion on evil-doers and to sympathise with those who are caught in the bonds of sin. It means to forego every self-righteousness and every self-justification in comparison with others. It means to refuse to condemn those who do wrong, but to forgive them. It is to say with utter seriousness, *"Forgive us our trespasses as we forgive those who trespass against us"* (Matthew 6:12).

According to Jesus, a spiritual person would be merciful if they know that they themselves are also sinful and in need of God's mercy. There is no one without sin; no one can claim righteousness before God. If one claims to have no sin, says Saint John, he is a liar, and makes God a liar as well (1 John 1:10, 2:4). The spiritual person, because he is in union with God, acknowledges his sin and his need for forgiveness from God and from men. They cannot condemn others for they know, if it were not for the grace of Christ, that they themselves would stand unworthy. King David affirms these words when he says, *"If You, Lord, should mark iniquities, O Lord, who could stand? But there is forgiveness with You, That You may be feared"* (Psalm 130:3-4).

The merciful person is merciful toward himself as well as others. This does not mean that he makes light of his sins and takes God's forgiveness for granted. It means rather, that he does not plague himself with neurotic guilt but trusts in the loving-kindness of God.

St. Paul says,

> *"For by grace you have been saved through faith; and this not your own doing, it is the gift of God—not because of works, lest any man boast. For we are His workmanship, created in Christ Jesus for good works, which God prepared beforehand, that we should walk in them"* (Ephesians 2:8–10)

Therefore, a merciful person knows, as St. Paul said, that no merit of his will deliver him from the need for God's mercy and love and so he too shows mercy to others.

Thus, it is the continual reception of the mercy of God and nothing else which empowers the soul to good works. And it is only the merciful who attain mercy from God. For all eternity man will be at the disposal of God's mercy. At whatever stage of spiritual progress he will reach, man's prayer will always remain to be, "Lord have mercy on me a sinner", as the church teaches! The holier the person, the greater he desires spiritual perfection, the stronger is his dependence on the mercy of God, and so the more he is merciful towards the weaknesses of others.

Purity in Heart

"Blessed are the pure in heart, for they shall see God" (Matthew 5:8)

Purity of heart means to be free of all sinful intentions, and to have no unworthy interests or self-seeking desires. It means to be totally free from anything which blinds and darkens the mind so that it cannot see spiritual matters clearly. It is, furthermore, to be totally liberated from anything which captivates the soul so that it cannot reflect the light of God.

In another section of Christ's Sermon on the Mountain, He says,

"The eye is the lamp of the body. So if your eye is sound, your body will be full of light; but if your eye is not sound, your whole body will be full of darkness. If then the light that is in you is darkness, how great is that darkness!" (Matthew 7:22–23)

The pure in heart are therefore those whose eyes are sound. If one desires purity, they are to shield their eyes from obscene things so as not to give room for darkness to enter their heart and entire being.

However, there are other elements involved too, as found in the Psalms. The pure in heart are those who can say with the psalmist,

> *"One thing I have desired of the Lord, That will I seek: That I may dwell in the house of the Lord All the days of my life, To behold the beauty of the Lord ... My heart said to You, "Your face, Lord, I will seek."*
> (Psalm 27:4,8)

That is, to seek the face of the Lord exclusively, is purity of heart. To will but one thing, the light of the Lord in the depth of one's soul, is to live in utter purity. It is for this reason that Christ's mother, Mary, is the image of perfect purity. The holy Virgin is "all-pure" not merely because of her bodily continence, but also because of her spiritual soundness. Her heart was pure, her soul magnified the Lord and her spirit rejoiced in God her Saviour. Her body was His spiritual temple. For this reason, God regarded her humility and did great things for her. This also explains why all generations call her blessed. For she, in her simple purity, could say to God: "Let it be to me according to your word" (Lk 1:38), when it was announced to her that she would become the mother of God.

In the spiritual tradition of the church, purity of heart is an essential condition for union with God. When man's heart is purified from all evil, it naturally shines with the light of God, since God dwells in the soul.

This is the doctrine of the saints as expressed by St. Gregory of Nyssa when he says,

> *"The man who purifies the eye of his soul will enjoy an immediate vision of God"*
> (On the Beatitudes, Sermon 6)

The Apostle Paul also said the same thing in his pastoral letters. In one instance he says,

"To the pure all things are pure, but to the corrupt and faithless nothing is pure ... They profess to know God, but they deny Him by their deeds" (Titus 1:15–16). And again he says,

"If anyone purifies himself from what is ignoble, then he will be a vessel of noble use, consecrated and useful to the master ... ready for any good work. So shun youthful passions and aim at righteousness, faith, love and peace, along with those who call upon the Lord from a pure heart" (2 Timothy 2:21–22).

Peacemakers

> *"Blessed are the peacemakers, for they shall be called sons of God"* (Matthew 5:9)

Christ, the "prince of peace," (Isaiah 9:6) gives the peace of God to those who believe in Him. He says,

"Peace I leave with you; My peace I give to you; not as the world gives do I give to you" (John 14:27) and again,

"I have said these things to you, that in Me you may have peace" (John 16:33).

This is the peace which St Paul lists as one of the "fruits of the Holy Spirit" (Galatians 5:22); the *"peace of God which passes all understanding"* (Philippians 4:7). It is peace understood as *"the liberation from passions, which cannot be attained without the action of the Holy Spirit"* (Saint Mark the Ascetic, 4th c., Two Centuries on Spiritual Law). The peacemakers are those who have the peace of God in themselves and spread this peace to those around them. This peace, first of all, is the freedom from all anxiety and fear. It is the peace of those who are not anxious about their lives, about what they shall eat and drink or about what they shall wear. It is the peace with which men's hearts are not troubled nor afraid of anything. It is moreover the peace which exists in men even in the most terrible of human situations, in suffering and in death. It is the peace which inhabits the one who can say,

> *"Who shall separate us from the love of Christ? Shall tribulation, or distress, or persecution, or famine, or nakedness, or peril, or sword?"* (Romans 8:35)

The blessed peacemaker is also the one who bears witness to Christ through his daily life by facing the challenges of his life without fear or anxiety. He is the one who does not exercise violence, but instead remains peaceful amidst conflict, and so points people towards Christ as a result. The peace which he possesses is noticeably *"not as the world gives"* (John 14:27).

> *"If possible, so far as it depends on you, live peaceably with all. Beloved, never avenge yourself, but leave it to the wrath of God, for it is written, 'Vengeance is Mine, I will repay,' says the Lord"* (Leviticus 19:18, Deuteronomy 32:35)

No, "if your enemy is hungry, feed him; if he is thirsty, give him drink; for by so doing you will heap burning coals upon his head" (Proverbs 25:21–22). "Do not be overcome by evil, but overcome evil with good" (Romans 12:18–21).

Thus, the peacemaker does not provoke others to irritation or violence and leaves all vengeance to the Lord as opposed to involving himself in strife. He is the one who follows Jesus in overcoming evil only by good.

Persecuted for Righteousness' Sake

> *"Blessed are they who are persecuted for righteousness' sake for theirs is the kingdom of heaven. Blessed are you when they revile and persecute you, and say all kinds of evil against you falsely for My sake"* (Matthew 5:10–11)

In saying these words, Christ promised that those who would follow Him would certainly be persecuted. This is a fundamental prediction of the Gospel and an essential condition.

Christ also said,

> *"Remember the word that I said to you, 'A servant is not greater than his master.' If they persecute Me, they will persecute you ... But all this they will do to you on My account, because they do not know Him who sent Me"* (John 15:20–21)

Therefore, true Christians will always be persecuted for Christ's sake. They will be persecuted with Christ and like Christ, for the truth that they speak and the good that they do. The persecutions may not always be physical, but they will always be spiritual and psychological. They will always be mindless, unjust, violent, and "without cause" (Psalm 69:4, John 15:25). This is affirmed by the verse, *"For indeed all who desire to live a godly life in Christ Jesus will be persecuted"* (2 Timothy 3:12).

A person embarking on the spiritual life must expect persecution and slander. He must be wary, however, of any false persecution complex, and must be absolutely certain that the suffering he meets is solely *"for righteousness' sake"* and not because of his own weaknesses and sins. The apostolic scripture makes this precise warning,

> *"For this is commendable, if because of conscience toward God one endures grief, suffering wrongfully. For what credit is it if, when you are beaten for your faults, you take it patiently? But when you do good and suffer, if you take it patiently, this is commendable before God. For to this you were called, because Christ also suffered for us, leaving us an example, that you should follow His steps ... If you are reproached for the name of Christ, blessed are you, for the Spirit of glory and of God rests upon you. On their part He is blasphemed, but on your part He is glorified. But let none of you suffer as a murderer, a thief, an evildoer, or as a busybody in other people's matters. Yet if anyone suffers as a Christian, let him not be ashamed, but let him glorify God in this matter."* (1 Peter 2:19–21, 4:14–16)

The suffering of Christians must be accepted gladly, with mercy and love to those who inflict it. Here once again is the Lord's own example, as well as that of His prophets, apostles, martyrs and saints. As Christ said, *"Father, forgive them"* (Luke 23:34), while hanging on the Cross; and as the first martyr Stephen prayed, *"Lord, do not hold this sin against them"* (Acts 7:60), while being stoned, so all those who follow God's righteousness must forgive their offenders "from [their] heart" (Matthew 18:35). Referring back to the Sermon on the Mountain,

> *"But I say to you that hear, Love your enemies, do good to those who hate you, bless those who curse you, pray for those who abuse you. To him who strikes you on the cheek, offer the other also; and from him who takes away your cloak do not withhold your coat as well ... Love your enemies, and do good, and give, expecting nothing in return, and your reward will be great, and you will be sons of the Most High; for He is kind to the ungrateful and selfish. Be merciful, even as your Father is merciful. Judge not, and you will not be judged; condemn not, and you will not be condemned; forgive, and you will be forgiven; give, and it will be given to you."* (Luke 6:27–38)

The loving forgiveness of the persecuted for the persecutors is an essential condition of the spiritual life. Without it, all suffering "for righteousness' sake" is in vain, and does not lead to the Kingdom of Heaven.

The Orthodox Creed

"Truly we believe in One God, the Almighty God the Father, maker of heaven and earth, of all things visible and invisible. We believe in one Lord, Jesus Christ the only begotten Son of God, born of the Father before all ages; light out of light, true God out of true God, begotten not made; consubstantial with the Father, through whom all things came into being.

He descended from heaven for us and for our salvation, and was incarnated from the Holy Spirit and of the Virgin Mary, and became man. He was crucified for us at the time of Pontius Pilate. He suffered and was buried; arose from the dead on the third day in accordance with the Scriptures; He ascended to the heavens and sat at the right hand of the Father; He shall also come in His glory to judge the living and the dead; of whose kingdom there will be no end.

Truly we believe in the Holy Spirit, the Life-giving Lord, who proceeds from the Father, we worship and glorify Him together with the Father and the Son, who spoke in the prophets. And in one, holy, universal and Apostolic Church. We acknowledge one baptism for the remission of sins. And we look for the resurrection of the dead and the life of the world to come. Amen."

We begin the Creed with "We believe." This is because the essence of our religious convictions depends not on external experiences but on our acceptance of God-given truths. Surely one cannot prove truths of the spiritual world by any laboratory experiments. These truths belong to the sphere of personal religious experience. The more a person grows in the spiritual life – the more one prays, thinks about God, does good – the more his inner spiritual experience develops, the clearer the religious truths become to him. In this fashion, faith becomes for him a subject of personal experience.

According to the Creed, we believe that God is one fullness of perfection; we believe that He is a perfect being, timeless, without beginning, all-powerful and all-wise. God is everywhere, sees all, and knows beforehand when something will happen. He is good beyond measure, just and all-holy. He needs nothing and is the reason for everything that exists.

We believe that God is one in Essence and Trinity in Persons. That is, the one true God has appeared to us as Father, Son, and Holy Spirit – as Trinity – yet one in Essence and indivisible.

We believe that all the Persons of the Holy Trinity are equal in divine perfection, greatness, power, and glory. That is, we believe that the Father is true and perfect God, the Son is true and perfect God, and, the Holy Spirit is true and perfect God. Therefore, in prayers, we simultaneously glorify the Father, the Son, and the Holy Spirit as one God.

We believe that the entire universe, both the visible and the invisible, was created by God. In the beginning God created the invisible, great angelic world, otherwise known as Heaven. As stated in the Bible, God created our material or physical world from nothing. This was not done at once, but gradually during periods of time which in the Bible are called "days." God created the world not out of necessity or need but out of His all-good desire to do so in order that His other creations might enjoy life. Being Himself endlessly good, God created all things good. Evil appeared in the world from the misuse of free will, with which God has endowed both angels and people. For example, the Devil (Satan) and his demons were at one time angels of God. But they rebelled against their Creator and became demons. They were cast out of Heaven and formed their own kingdom called "hell". From that moment on, they tempted people to sin and became the enemies of our salvation.

We believe that all things are under God's control; that is, He provides for every creature and guides everything to a good goal. God loves and looks after us as a mother looks after her child. For this reason, nothing bad can befall a person who trusts in God – even when it appears to be bad. We read in Romans 8:28, "And we know that all things work together for good, to those who love God, to those who are the called according to His purpose."

We believe that the Son of God, our Lord Jesus Christ, came down from heaven for our salvation. He came to earth and took on our flesh by the Holy Spirit and the Virgin Mary. Being God from all eternity, He in the time of King Herod took on our human nature, both soul and body, and is therefore truly God and truly man, or the God-man. In one divine Person He united two natures, divine and human. These two natures will remain with Him always without change, neither blending nor changing from one into the other.

We believe that our Lord Jesus Christ, while living on earth, enlightened the world by His teaching, His example, and miracles. He taught people what they should believe and how they should live so that they may inherit eternal life. By His suffering and crucifixion on the cross, He defeated the devil and redeemed the world from sin and death. By His Resurrection from the dead, He laid the foundation for our resurrection. After His Ascension in the flesh to Heaven, which took place forty days after His Resurrection from the dead, our Lord Jesus Christ sat at the right hand of God the Father; that is to say, in equal power with God the Father, governing the face of the world with Him.

We believe that our Lord Jesus Christ, while living on earth, enlightened the world by His teaching

We believe that the Holy Spirit, preceding from God the Father before the beginning of the world, together with the Father and the Son gives existence to all creation, gives life, and governs all. We read, "But when the Helper comes, whom I shall send to you from the Father, the Spirit of truth who proceeds from the Father, He will testify of Me" (John 15:26). The Holy Spirit is the source of a grace-filled spiritual life, both for angels as well as people. Being true and perfect God equally with the Father and the Son, He is worthy of all glory and worship. The Holy Spirit spoke in the Old Testament through the prophets and then at the beginning of the New Testament spoke through the Apostles, and now lives in the Church of Christ, guiding her pastors and people in the truth.

We believe that our Lord Jesus Christ founded the Church on earth for the salvation of all who believe in Him. He sent the Holy Spirit to the Apostles on Pentecost. Since that time the Holy Spirit abides in the Church, that grace-filled community or union of believing Orthodox Christians, and preserves her in the purity of Christ's teaching. The grace of the Holy Spirit abides in the Church, cleanses those who repent of sins, helps the believers grow in good deeds, and sanctifies them.

We believe that the Church is One, Holy, Catholic and Apostolic. She is One because all Orthodox Christians, although belonging to different national and local churches, are one family together with the angels and saints in Heaven. The oneness of the Church depends on oneness of Faith and Grace. The Church is Holy because her faithful children are sanctified by the word of God, prayer, and the Sacraments (which will be explained in the coming section). The Church is Catholic because what we believe is the same teaching held to be true by all Orthodox Christians, always and everywhere. The Church is called Apostolic because it preserves Apostolic teaching and the Apostolic succession. From ancient times, this Apostolic succession passes on without interruption from Bishop to Bishop in the sacrament of Ordination. The Church of our Lord and Saviour will remain until the end of time.

We believe that in the sacrament of Baptism the believer is forgiven all sins. The believer becomes a member of the Church and a son of God, able to call out to Him as "Father". Access to the other sacraments of salvation becomes available to them at this time. In the sacrament of Chrismation, the believer receives the Holy Spirit. In Repentance and Confession, sins are forgiven. In Holy Communion, offered at the Divine Liturgy, the believer receives the very Body and Blood of Christ. In the sacrament of Matrimony, an inseparable union is created between a man and a woman. In the sacrament of Ordination, Deacons, Priests, and Bishops are ordained to serve the Church. In Holy Unction, the healing of physical and spiritual illness is offered.

We believe that at the end of the world Jesus Christ, accompanied by angels, will again come to the earth in glory. Every person will resurrect from the dead and a miracle will occur, in which the souls of people who have died will return into the bodies which they possessed during their earthly life. All the dead will come to life. During the General Resurrection, the bodies of the saints, both those resurrecting and those still living will be renewed and become spiritualised in the image of the Resurrected Body of Christ. After the resurrection, everyone will appear before the Judgment of Christ, to receive what they are due, according to what they have done when they lived in their body, whether good or evil. After the Judgment, unrepentant sinners will enter into eternal torments and the righteous into eternal life. This will begin the Kingdom of Christ, which will have no end.

With the concluding word "Amen", we witness to the fact that we accept and acknowledge with our whole heart this Creed which we confess to be true.

The Creed is read by a catechumen (one about to receive baptism) during the Sacrament of Baptism. During the baptism of an infant, the Creed is read by the parents. The Creed is recited at the liturgy and should be read daily at Morning Prayers. An attentive reading of the Creed greatly strengthens our faith. This happens because the Creed is not just a formal statement of belief but a prayer. When we say "I believe" in a spirit of prayer, along with the other words of the Creed, we enliven and strengthen our Faith in God and in all those truths which are contained in the Creed. This is why it is so important for the Orthodox Christian to recite the Creed daily or at least regularly.

Introduction to the Coptic Orthodox Church

The Coptic Church was established in the name of the Lord Jesus Christ by St. Mark the Evangelist in the city of Alexandria around 43 A.D. The church adheres to the Nicene Creed. St. Athanasius (296-373 A.D.), the twentieth Pope of the Coptic Church effectively defended the Doctrine of the Lord Jesus Christ's Divinity at the Council of Nicea in 325 A.D. His affirmation of the doctrine earned him the titles, St. Athanasius the "Father of Orthodoxy" and St. Athanasius the "Apostolic".

The term "Coptic" is derived from the Greek "Aigyptos" meaning "Egyptian". When the Arabs arrived in Egypt in the seventh century, they called the Egyptians "qibt". Thus, the Arabic word "qibt" came to mean both "Egyptians" and "Christians".

The term "Orthodoxy" here refers to the preservation of the "Original Faith" throughout the ages, as the Creed was defended against the numerous attacks aimed at it.

The Coptic Orthodox Church believes that the Holy Trinity: God the Father, God the Son, and God the Holy Spirit, are equal to each other in one unity; and that the Lord Jesus Christ is the only Saviour of the world.

Less changes have taken place in the Coptic Church than in any other church whether in the ritual or doctrinal aspects over the centuries. Moreover, the succession of the Coptic patriarchs, bishops, priests and deacons has been continuous.

The Coptic Church is ancient and new at the same time. It is ancient in that it is apostolic, founded by St. Mark the Evangelist and traditional in holding fast to the original apostolic faith without deviation. She is also new through her Living Messiah who never becomes old and through the Spirit of God who renews her youth (Psalm 103:5). It is a church that is rich with her evangelistic and ascetic life, her genuine patriotic inheritance, her heavenly worship, her spiritual rituals, her effective and living hymns and her beautiful icons. She attracts the heart towards heaven without ignoring actual daily life. We can say that she is an apostolic, contemporary church that carries life and thought to the contemporary man without deviation. One finds in her life, sweetness and power

She attracts the heart towards heaven without ignoring actual daily life

of Spirit, alongside an appreciation of arts, literature and human culture.

Isaiah 19:25 says, "Blessed is Egypt my people."

God's promise to His people is always fulfilled; He foretold that He would come to Egypt where it says, "and in that day there will be an altar to the Lord in the midst of the land of Egypt, and a pillar to the Lord at its border" (Isaiah 19:19). This promise was fulfilled by the flight of the Holy Family from the face of the tyrant Herod to find refuge elsewhere. Thus our Lord Jesus Christ came during His childhood to Egypt to lay by Himself the foundation stone of His church in Egypt which has become one of the four primary "Sees" in the world, among the churches of Jerusalem, Antioch and Rome, and joined later by the See of Constantinople (where a See is an area of a bishop's ecclesiastical jurisdiction).

The star of the Coptic Church shone through the School of Alexandria which taught the Christian world the allegoric and spiritual methods in interpreting the

Holy Scripture. The Coptic Church was also a leader in defending the Orthodox faith on an ecumenical level.

The Christian monastic movement in all its forms also started in Egypt, attracting the heart of the church towards the desert, to practise the angelic inner life.

Our church carried our Lord Jesus Christ's cross throughout generations, bearing numerous sufferings and persecutions. She continued to offer a countless number of martyrs and confessors throughout the ages (a martyr is someone who shed their blood after refusing to deny their faith in Christ; and a confessor is someone who witnessed to the faith and was tortured for it). Those who struggled to win the crowns of martyrdom did so happily and with hearts full of joy.

The Church is well known for her numerous saints, who consist of ascetics, clergymen and laymen. She produced many saints over the years and still does the same today. Those who follow the teachings of the church and diligently practise the sanctified life of communion with God can also reach such levels of holiness.

The Holy Sacraments

The Church Sacraments are sacred actions by which the believers receive invisible graces, through material or visible prayers. The Coptic Church observes seven sacraments:

1. Sacrament of Baptism

The Sacrament of Baptism is like the door by which the believer enters the church and has the right to partake in the rest of the Sacraments. At Baptism, we are spiritually reborn by being immersed in water three times in the name of the Holy Trinity; the Father, the Son and the Holy Spirit. The Lord Jesus Christ instituted the Sacrament of Baptism by being baptised by St. John the Baptist in the River Jordan, when the Holy Spirit came upon Him in the form of a dove. Then, Jesus assured it after His resurrection when He said to His disciples, "Go therefore and make disciples of all nations, baptising them in the name of the Father and of the Son and of the Holy Spirit" (Matthew: 28:19)

2. Sacrament of Confirmation

The Sacrament of Confirmation is also known as the Holy Anointment of Myron (The word 'Myron' is a Greek word which means 'ointment' or 'fragrant'). The baptised person receives the Holy Myron immediately after Baptism, so as to become a temple of the Holy Spirit. The Baptised is anointed with 36 signs of the cross on his head, chest, back and joints so that the Holy Spirit can dwell within them. The significance of anointing all these parts of the body is that they may each be sanctified for God – for example, anointing the eyes signifies that the eyes should be used in a way that is pleasing to God and not for judging others or indulging in impurity; anointing the joints as another example, signifies that all movements should likewise be for the glory of God. By this anointment, God grants the grace of confirmation to the baptised as well as the power of the Holy Spirit.

3. Sacrament of Confession and Repentance

The Sacrament of Repentance and Confession is a holy sacrament, by which the sinner returns to God, confessing their sins before God in the presence of the priest, to be absolved by the priest through the authority granted to him by God. By this absolution, the confessing person is granted the forgiveness of those sins which he confessed. This is in fact an authority given by Christ Himself, passed down from the apostles. Let's refer to John 20:23 in which Christ addresses the apostles saying, "Receive the Holy Spirit. If you forgive the sins of any, they are forgiven them; if you retain the sins of any, they are retained."

The next chapter contains more details on how to practise the sacrament of confession.

4. Sacrament of Holy Eucharist

The Sacrament of Communion is a Holy Sacrament by which the believer eats the Holy Body and drinks the Precious Blood of Jesus Christ, presented in the form of Bread and Wine. This Sacrament has a special significance among the Seven Church sacraments. It is sometimes called the 'Mystery of Mysteries' or the 'Crown of Sacraments'; for all the Sacraments are crowned by the Eucharist. The Lord Jesus instituted the holy Eucharist on Covenant Thursday (the day of the Last Supper). After He celebrated the Rite of Passover of the Jews (which was in commemoration of the Old Testament event where Moses and the Jews passed through the Red Sea to escape from the tyranny of Pharaoh at the time), He rose and washed the feet of His disciples, as a sign of repentance and preparation, then sat down and instituted the Passover of the New Covenant, which is the Sacrament of Holy Communion.

It says,

> *"He took bread, blessed it and broke it, and gave it to the disciples and said, 'Take, eat, this is My Body', then He took the cup and gave thanks, and gave it to His disciples saying, 'Drink from it, all of you, for this is My Blood of the New Covenant, which is shed for many for the remission of sins'" (Matthew 26:26-28).*

It is worthy to note that the word "Eucharist" comes from the Greek word "efcharistia", which means thanksgiving. That is, we ought to partake of this sacrament with thanksgiving towards Christ who offers us His own Body and Blood in order that we may have eternal life.

5. Sacrament of the Unction of the Sick

The Sacrament of the Unction of the Sick is one of the Seven Sacraments of the church, in which the priest and congregation pray for the sick to be healed from psychological and physical diseases, as well as spiritual weaknesses. The priest anoints the person with the holy oil, in supplication that they obtain the grace of remedy from God.

6. Sacrament of Holy Matrimony

Matrimony is a holy sacrament, officiated by a priest, of uniting a male and a woman to each other. Through this holy sacrament, the man and woman become one, for as the Lord Jesus said,

> *"For this reason a man shall leave his father and mother and be joined to his wife and the two shall become one flesh. So then, they are no longer two but one flesh. Therefore what God has joined together, let not man separate"* (Matthew 19:5, 6).

7. Sacrament of Priesthood

The Sacrament of Priesthood is a holy sacrament through which the bishop lays his hands on the head of the elected candidate, so that the Holy Spirit will descend on him and grant him one of the priestly ranks. He therefore receives the gifts of the Holy Spirit and is given the authority to officiate the Sacraments of the church, teach doctrine, and fulfill a pastoral role towards the congregation. The word "priest" is derived from the Greek word "Presbuteros", meaning the person in authority by the church who prays for others.

How to Confess?

Before the Confession

The most important part of confession takes place well before we even arrive at church. The sacrament is only as strong as the preparation we do in advance. Preparation is achieved by having regular times of self-examination and repentance.

Repentance is usually thought of as being a part of the confession process. However, the opposite is true. Repentance is not part of confession but it is rather confession that is part of repentance. Confession needs to take place regularly – at least every 2 months. On the other hand, repentance needs to take place daily. The goal is that repentance is not an activity, but rather a lifestyle.

This happens by making time for regular daily self-examination. As mentioned earlier, our confession will only be as strong as our investment in this practice of daily self-examination.

Going to Confession

We should try to get in the habit of confessing every 6-8 weeks. This can be made easier for us by setting regular times of confession. The sacrament of Confession should be treated the same way as the sacrament of the Eucharist – as a necessary part of the spiritual life that can be obtained at regular times.

After Confession

After we have received the absolution from the priest for the sins that have been confessed, some time needs to be spent at the church to pray and to thank God for carrying our sins.

It is advised that we also practise the 'prayer before and after confession' found at the end of the book of 'Agpeya' (the Coptic Orthodox Book of Prayers).

Choosing a Father of Confession

The Orthodox concept of confession has always stressed the importance of a father of confession. Confession is not just an impersonal listing of sins but is rather a part of a relationship of fatherhood & discipleship. It does not matter who the father of confession is, but we need to choose one and stick with him – even when he does not tell us what we

How to Confess?

want to hear. We can have several spiritual fathers but only one father of confession, as St. Paul said, "For though you might have ten thousand instructors in Christ, yet you do not have many fathers" (1 Corinthians 4:15).

Everyone must pray for their father of confession daily. This is a must. If we want him to be God's mouthpiece in our life, then we must pray that God guides him and gives him the spirit of wisdom and prophecy and the spirit of discernment to guide him. In addition, praying for our father of confession will help to establish the spiritual bond of love and fatherhood needed for this relationship to be fruitful.

Saints and Martyrs Inspire the Faith Today

A continual reminder that we are all called to be saints comes when we read St. Paul's letters to the early churches, addressed to "beloved of God, called to be saints," (Romans 1:7) and to those "who are sanctified in Christ Jesus, called to be saints" (1 Corinthians 1:2). We are thus all called to be saints. The Bible is clear that we are called to live holy lives. What then is holy living?

The Orthodox Church encourages the faithful to live a life of purity and repentance, reminding them of the lives of the desert fathers and mothers of the early Church. When we recall the lives of those who lived saintly lives before us, we are encouraged to do likewise. The saints are thus examples to direct and guide the faithful to holy and pure lives. This is achieved by reflection on the saint's life of piety, their words, and their actions and deeds. This is an exercise that should be done by everyone, both laity and clergy. Each saint provides an example of a virtue, a Christian principle, a Biblical teaching, a model of repentance and a holy life.

The word "saint" first appears in the Bible in the Book of Psalms, in Psalm 116 verse 15, "Precious in the sight of the Lord is the death of His saints." The Orthodox Church treasures the saints in its worship and devotion. Orthodox churches have an iconostasis at the front facing the people. The iconostases are the icons of the twelve Apostles, St Mary the Theotokos (which means "God-bearer"), and the Heavenly Hosts – Archangel Gabriel, the announcer of Christ's birth to St Mary, and the patron saints of the church. The iconostasis represents the door of heaven. Other icons of the saints and martyrs are displayed all around the perimeter of the church.

Generally, at the entrance of an Orthodox church the faithful lights a candle in front of St Mary the Theotokos or the patron saint of that church. They make their supplication and requests to God through the intercessions of the saint for their personal matters, who lift the prayers to God on their behalf. Many miracles and instances of healing occur as a result of the prayers of the saints, which is supported by James 5:16, "the effective, fervent prayer of a righteous man avails much". These saints are the righteous people this verse refers to, and hence their prayers avail much before God. The relics of saints or martyrs may be found in many Orthodox churches, as a source of blessing.

On entering the home of an Orthodox family, one will find icons of the saints and martyrs who were persecuted, tortured and finally killed because of their tremendous love for their God and Saviour Jesus Christ. In the early Church, icons were used as a means of educating the faithful by telling the story of the saint and their virtues. Just as a picture paints a thousand words, so the icon speaks eloquently of the holiness and presence of God in the life of the person portrayed. Many Orthodox homes also burn a continual oil lantern before their favourite saint or intercessor, as a sign of honour. The faithful truly believe that having an icon of our Lord Jesus Christ, St. Mary the Mother of God, or their favourite patron saint or martyr, provides blessings and protection to the home and its occupants.

Orthodox churches have their own process for discerning and nominating saints, also known as canonisation. In our own Coptic Orthodox tradition, 50 years must elapse after the candidate's death to distance the process from people's emotional attachment to the person. Then an application to the Holy Synod (a team of bishops lead by the Patriarch of the church) is made, presenting the whole life of the person, their virtues, holiness, teachings, and miracles that may have been performed during their life and since their death. Photographs, letters, correspondence, attestations of miracles are all included. If the application is clear cut, the subcommittee will recommend sainthood. If not, further enquiries and investigation may be required. The most recently canonised saints of the Coptic Orthodox Church are His Holiness Pope Cyril VI (also known as Pope Kyrillos VI), who passed away in 1971 (with an exception to the 50 year rule being applied due to the overwhelmingly strong evidence of his sainthood), and Archdeacon Habib Guirguis, who departed in 1951.

However, a martyr who lays down his life for Christ is automatically called a saint. During the Christian persecution under the reign of the Roman Emperor Diocletian, more than one million Egyptian Coptic Christians were martyred. In 284AD, St Peter the Seal of Martyrs recommenced the Coptic New Calendar (which comprised of the ancient Egyptian calendar of twelve months of thirty days, and a short month of five days) in memory of Diocletian's era of martyrs, considering that year the beginning of the Coptic Calendar. This was because of the strong belief that "the blood of the martyrs is the seed of the church", as coined by Tertullian, a church father.

The Coptic Orthodox Church is a church rich with martyrs, to the extent that it is said that Egypt's soil is soaked with their blood. The Coptic New Year is a time when the Church remembers all such martyrs and saints, commemorated on 11 September each year. Every day, the Church reminds the faithful of the witness of the martyrs and saints through a book with the chronology of saints, called the Synaxarium. On the first of Tut (the first Coptic month), the Church issues a calendar with the dates of departure of such saints, encouraging the congregation to commemorate them on those days, as is done in the Holy Liturgy each day.

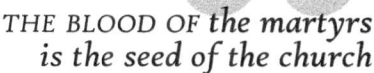

*THE BLOOD OF **the martyrs** is the seed of the church*

Saints and martyrs from the period prior to the separation of the Eastern and Western churches in 451AD are shared by the universal Church. First among them is St Mary the Mother of God. She is loved by all because she conceived through the Holy Spirit and gave birth to Jesus Christ the Son of God, and yet remained a perpetual virgin. St Mary is a model of humility, meekness, simplicity, purity and holiness, and her continual intercessions on behalf of humanity before her Son Jesus Christ is cherished by the Orthodox faithful. Other common saints of the early Church include St Antony the Great, the father of monastic life, and St Athanasius of Alexandria, the 20th Pope of Alexandria and of the See of St Mark, who was instrumental in shaping the Nicene Creed of the 4th Century (which is professed by all churches in the world today).

Generally, churches value each other's saints, and Orthodox churches have regard for the saints that have been declared by other churches. Orthodox faithful though have a special interest in the stories of the martyrs, and the fathers and mothers of the Egyptian desert, whose writings such as The Sayings of the Desert Fathers, The Philokalia, and Vita Antony are filled with practical sayings and life experience. Along with our sister Orthodox churches, the Coptic Orthodox Church welcomes the Catholic Church's canonisation of Mary MacKillop to be the first saint for Australia. All Australians will love St. Mary MacKillop for her love in educating the poor. Australia is founded by great people such as Mary MacKillop, who dedicated her life to service and prayer for the sake of others. We ask for her prayers and intercessions, and for the intercessions of Our Mother St Mary the Mother of God, to intercede on behalf of all Australians and all the people of the world.

Raising Children to be Children of God

Children are a gift from God, as it is written in the Psalms, "Behold, children are a heritage from the Lord, the fruit of the womb is a reward" (Psalm 127:3). Parents have a responsibility towards their children, as St. Paul wrote, "And you, fathers, do not provoke your children to wrath, but bring them up in the training and admonition of the Lord" (Ephesians 6:4). God told the Israelites to teach their children His commandments,

> *"And these words which I command you today shall be in your heart. You shall teach them diligently to your children, and shall talk of them when you sit in your house, when you walk by the way, when you lie down, and when you rise up"* (Deuteronomy 6:6-7)

St. Paul praised his disciple Timothy and his genuine faith, which dwelt first in his grandmother then in his mother. He wrote, "I call to remembrance the genuine faith that is in you, which dwelt first in your grandmother Lois and your mother Eunice, and I am persuaded is in you also" (2 Timothy 1:5).

Raising children in the fear of God, passing on to them the Orthodox faith, and making them become children of God is a very important matter. Raising them in a spiritual way is a holy duty to which the parents will have to give an account for on Judgment Day. God will ask every father and mother regarding their children and whether they carried out their necessary responsibility towards them. Will every father and mother be able to stand in front of God and say, "Here am I and the children whom the Lord has given me" (Isaiah 8:18)? The salvation of every father and mother is directly related to the salvation of his or her children. There are many parents whom the Lord punished, because they neglected their duty in raising their children. Eli the priest offers us the perfect example. Although he was a righteous man, yet the Lord punished him

> GOD WILL ASK *every father and mother regarding their children*

because of his children's evil actions, since he did not raise them well (refer to 1 Samuel 2).

The church exhorts parents to place great care in the upbringing of their children, reminding them that the virtuous Christian home is the fruitful environment in which upright children can be brought forth. The following section will include some advice and guidelines regarding effective Christian child rearing, using the writings of St. John Chrysostom the bishop of Constantinople, as the foundation for this.

The Goal of Raising Children

Parents have a responsibility to raise their children properly. The goal of their upbringing must be clear from the beginning. St. John Chrysostom specifies this goal to be making the child become God's child. He compares the parents' task to that of a sculptor. The parents must be firm guides and zealous criticisers so as to shape the child to become the Lord's child. According to St. John, parents are like,

> *"ones who make statues, removing the excess and correcting the imperfections. They examine their children day after day to see what virtues they acquired so as to instil more of it and what shortcomings they have so as to remove."*

He also said,

> *"We have to care for these beautiful statues in our hands to shape them for the sake of God. They are not hard and inanimate, but the King of the universe has desired to dwell in them. Therefore, let us use God's words to form the child, because you raise a philosopher (a godly wise person) or a hero racing towards the Kingdom of God to become a heavenly citizen."*

The Importance of Discipline from Early Childhood

Proper discipline must start in early childhood as the young child is more easily taught. The sooner we start teaching them to live a Christian life, the better we will be at achieving our goal. St. John Chrysostom said, "If the good commandments are imprinted on the soul while it is still young, then no one can destroy it … The child still has fear and awe in his sight, his speech, and in everything else." He also stated,

> *"It is easy to lead him since he doesn't have to struggle for honour or greatness, because he is still a child. He doesn't have a wife or children. What reason does he have to be arrogant or to speak evil? He competes only with his peers."*

Raising Children to be Children of God

The home in a way becomes a small church in which the child develops. It is within this setting that passing down the faith to the child is an important and decisive matter. There is the example of Moses the prophet, whose mother nursed him with faith in God. Consequently, all the idolatries in Pharaoh's castle did not make him forget his ancestors' faith (after he was taken from his mother). Because of his saintly mother and her righteous upbringing of him, he himself became a hero of faith. St. Paul wrote, "By faith Moses, when he became of age, refused to be called the son of Pharaoh's daughter, choosing rather to suffer affliction with the people of God than to enjoy passing pleasures of sin" (Hebrew 11:24-25).

St. John Chrysostom presents to parents a comprehensive program to teach their children the principles of the faith. He wrote, "Teach your child a chapter of the Bible with all its facts and meanings." For the young child, he advises that one should start with the attractive and happy stories. He specifies dinnertime as a suitable time for narrating the story step by step, using simple and easy phrases, without any additions to the facts, so that it wouldn't seem like a fable. If both parents are present, then one should tell the story, while the other comments on the events – that way teaching the child becomes a joint parent effort. We should not worry if the child does not understand one of the words or phrases, because they will understand the overall meaning from our facial expression and tone of voice. Repeat the story several times in one sitting, then allow the child to recount it. If they show signs of inability to retell it, help them by reminding them of some of the elements so that they can recollect it and repeat it. St. John also advises that it is important to apply the events of the story to the child's daily life. He wrote, "If the story has a deep meaning, then its significance will fill them with awe and admiration."

As the child gets older, St. John calls for gradually teaching the child more. The simple and happy stories are taught at a young age. When they are older, present to them deeper meanings. St. John wrote, "Afterwards, when the child grows, you can tell them stories, which inspire divine respect and fear. When they are young, you cannot overwhelm them, because they are still fragile."

Naming the Child

St. John Chrysostom gives special importance to naming children after the names of saints, so that from their early childhood the child becomes attached to that saint they are named after. The family should then celebrate this saint's feast day in a way similar to celebrating the child's birthday. St. John advises the parents to give the child an icon of the saint so that the child can become familiar with them. This would also encourage the child to imitate the saint, who was a true disciple of our Lord Jesus Christ, rather than taking fictional characters, movie stars, or sport athletes as role models.

St. John wrote,

> "Let the image of a saint be imprinted on the child by one way or another. Let us provide the child with opportunities to allow them to escalate in goodness by means of the name they are given. Let us not give the child the name of one of the family members, but rather the name of one of the righteous martyrs, apostles, or saints. This way we start caring for our children and instructing them, as well as introducing the saints' names into our homes. As a result, the parents will also meditate on the life of the saint, whose name they have given to their child. If the saint's name happens to be the same like a departed relative, then as both the parents and the child meditate on the life of this saint and pray with him, they will find comfort in losing their relative."

This illustrates the importance of the role the parents play in raising their children in a Christian way, whose goal is making the child truly a child of God. This has to start from early childhood. In fact, it should begin at the moment the infant is given a name. Connecting the child from his early life to the character of the saint they are named after imprints the saint's life on the child. Child rearing is a continuous process and must follow a calculated method so that, according to their developmental age, the child will gradually grow in the faith.

Monasticism

Monasticism began in the Coptic Orthodox Church towards the end of the third century, and flourished in the fourth. There were hundreds of monasteries and thousands of caves in the mountains of Egypt. It is said that if one were to travel from Alexandria in the North of Egypt to Luxor in the South, they would hear the sounds of the prayers, hymns and praises of the monks scattered in the desert along the whole journey. For the monks, monasticism was the life of prayer, contemplation, solitude, worship and purity of heart. They had nothing in their minds, hearts and feelings except God alone. They lived the calm and quiet life, abiding in the Lord, detaching themselves from everything and everyone, to be attached to Him alone.

Forms of Monasticism

Monasticism took three main forms, all of which are still to be found in the Church today,

❖ Monarchism

The anchorites or hermits lived in complete seclusion, only visiting the abbot when they needed counsel. Each hermit organised his own prayer, clothing, food and work. The first anchorite in the world was Saint Paul. He lived for eighty years in the Egyptian desert without seeing a single person.

❖ The Coenobitic System

Under this system founded by Saint Pachomius in Upper Egypt, the monks lived in a community inside the walls of the monastery being governed by an abbot. Even through this system, Christian monasticism never lost its yearning for monarchism.

❖ The Communal System or Semi-eremitic Life

This form of monasticism is mid-way between monarchism and the coenobitic system. The mode of St. Anthony's life as described by St. Athanasius was actually semi-eremitic in essence, for the monks lived in separate caves or cells and assembled occasionally for the Divine Liturgy or spiritual meetings. Thus, St. Anthony prepared the way for the communal order. In the wildernesses of Nitria and Scetis, the communal order was established by St. Amoun and St. Macarius the Great. There, the ascetics lived not in absolute isolation but in cells built at such a distance that they could neither see nor hear one another. They gathered for communal prayer on Saturdays and Sundays.

Monasticism's Famous Personalities

As referred to earlier, St. Paul the Anchorite (234 – 342 AD) was the first hermit. In 250 AD, he inherited great wealth upon the death of his parents when he was 16 years old. He fled to the desert where he lived over eighty years. Each day a raven would bring him half a loaf of bread. His biography was written by St. Jerome in 374 AD.

St. Anthony (251 – 356 AD) was eighteen years old when he entered the church and heard the words of the Gospel, "If you want to be perfect, go, sell all you have and give to the poor; and come, follow Me " (Matthew 19:21). He sold his land, entrusted his sister with a community of virgins, and lived in a hut under the guidance of a recluse. He visited Alexandria in 316 AD to assist the martyrs and in 352 AD to help St. Athanasius in his fight against Arianism.

St. Pachomius (292 – 348 AD) was converted to Christianity in Upper Egypt, when he witnessed the generosity of Christians and their love even of their enemies. He left the army and was baptised in 307

AD, becoming a disciple of Palamon the Hermit. He established the Coenobitic System. He founded two monasteries in Egypt, and two nunneries under the guidance of his sister. He laid the coenobitic laws which were later translated into Greek and Latin and used by St. Basil the Great.

St. Macarius the Great (300-390 AD) founded the communal order in the desert of Scetis, and visited St. Anthony at least twice.

St. Shenouda the Archimandrite ('Head of the Anchorites') was the abbott of the 'White Monastery' located in Upper Egypt for more than 65 years (in the 4th and 5th centuries), leading 2,200 monks and 1,800 nuns. In 431 AD, he accompanied St. Cyril the Great to the Ecumenical Council of Ephesus.

St. Sarah the Abbess was endowed with the grace of true leadership and spiritual discernment. Her sayings were treasured by the desert fathers.

St. Syncletica founded the first monastic community for women in the world in Alexandria. Her biography and teachings were preserved by Pope Athanasius.

Effects of Coptic Monasticism on the World

Coptic Monasticism is considered the most profound spiritual revival in the history of the Church. The news of the spiritual life of the monks spread everywhere. They did not write about themselves as there is no Coptic published history about the Coptic monks. People came from all around the world in order to hear a word of benefit from one of the monks, and to take it as a word of spiritual guidance. St. Palladius visited many monks and wrote his famous book, the 'Paradise of the Fathers', from which we learn about these holy fathers, who neither spoke nor wrote, but kept silent. They were not preachers but they were living sermons, examples of the true life and the image of God on earth.

A Short List of The Influence of These Saints

1. Pope Athanasius was greatly responsible for the introduction of the monastic movement to the Roman religious life, during his exile in Treve and his flight to Rome in 339 AD. He also wrote 'The Life of Anthony', read and translated all over the world.

2. The Pachomian rules were translated into Greek by Palladius, and into Latin by St. Jerome.

3. St. John Cassian (360 - 435 AD) dwelt in Egypt amongst the monks for seven years, and wrote his two famous books, "Institutes" and "Conferences".

4. Evagrius Ponticus, who occupied a central role in the history of Christian spirituality lived as a monk

for two years in Nitria, one of the earliest Christian monastic sites in Egypt and then fourteen years at a location called 'The Cells'.

6. St. Jerome and St. Rufinus visited Egypt.

7. St. Hilarious of Palestine became a disciple of St. Anthony in Egypt and returned to his own land to practice ascetiscm.

8. Etheria (Egaria), a Spanish abbess in the fourth century, visited Egypt.

9. St. Melania the elder, a Roman lady, visited the desert of Egypt.

10. St. John Chrysostom stayed in one of the Pachomian monasteries for 8 years.

11. Orphenus came to Egypt and wrote 'The Desert Fathers'.

12. St. Epiphanius (315 – 403 AD), Bishop of Salamis in Cyprus, was instructed in Coptic monastic thought.

A Brief Word on Mission & Evangelism in the Church

Organised groups, individuals, monks, clergymen, merchants, soldiers and devout women from Egypt went out to almost every part of the world and spread the Gospel. The School of Alexandria sent out missionaries to pagan tribes in Libya, Phrygia, Sinai, Arabia Felix, the Thebaid and Upper Egypt. Pantaenus especially is well-known for his work in India. Christianity was first introduced into Ethiopia by Egyptian merchants through their commercial and maritime relations, and into Sudan in the 6th century.

In Europe, St. Athanasius founded a church in Belgium during one of his exiles. In Switzerland, the Theban Legion led by St. Maurice, watered the land with the blood of their martyrdom when they refused to sacrifice to the gods; hence the place was named St. Moritz. Felix, his sister and their friend spread the Gospel in Zurich, and the official seal of the country of Zurich still bears the picture of these three Coptic evangelists. In Ireland, seven Coptic monks were among the pioneers of the faith, and left many traces in the life and art of the people; three manuscripts in the Royal Academy of Dublin confirm this.

www.ingramcontent.com/pod-product-compliance
Lightning Source LLC
LaVergne TN
LVHW041254080426
835510LV00009B/737